Understanding Contracts for Entrepreneurs

Understanding Contracts for Entrepreneurs for entrepreneurs and managers faced with navigating the complexities of contract negotiation and drafting. This text creates awareness of legal issues in contracting by using common-language explanations and everyday examples to explain otherwise complex contract law topics.

Please visit www.TheBusinessProfessor.com for additional legal and business resources.

TABLE OF QUESTIONS

CHAPTER 1: INTRODUCTION TO CONTRACTS

Overview

Why is it important for entrepreneurs and managers to understand contracts?

What is a Contract?

Do the parties to a contract have to understand the rules of contract?

What exactly is contract law and from where does it originate?

How is common law created?

How do legislators come up with statutory law?

What is the Restatement of Contract?

What is the Article 2 of the Uniform Commercial Code?

Why is there a distinction between individuals and merchants under the UCC?

CHAPTER 2: ANATOMY OF A CONTRACT

Introduction

What are the terms of a contract?

What are the benefits of a written contract?

Anatomy of a Written Contract

What are the major components of a written contract?

What is the preamble to a written contract?

What are the recitals?

What are the words of agreement?

What are the definitions and why are they included?

What is the action section?

What are representations and warranties?

What are covenants?

What are conditions?

What are the endgame provisions?

What are the general provisions?

What is the signature block?

CHAPTER 3: FORMING A CONTRACT: THE OFFER

Overview

What is an express contract?

What is an implied-in-fact contract?

What is an Implied-in-Law or Quasi-Contract?

Elements of a Contract

The Offer

What is an offer?

When is a communication or promise by one party not an offer?

Who can be an offeror?

How specific must the offer be?

When does the offer go into effect?

Once an offer is made, how long does it last?

So, by what means can an offer close or be terminated?

How do you revoke an offer?

Can all offers by revoked?

When is the revocation effective?

Are the rules of offer and acceptance the same when dealing with automated ordering and fulfillment systems?

CHAPTER 4: FORMING A CONTRACT: THE ACCEPTANCE

How do you accept an offer?

What is a bilateral and unilateral contract and how does it affect acceptance?

Can an offeror revoke a unilateral offer after the offeree begins performance, but has not completed?

What if the offeree does not respond to the offer?

What if an offeree does not respond to the offer but accepts deliver of the goods or services?

After acceptance, can a failure to communicate acceptance to the offeror prejudice the offeree?

In a unilateral contract, does the offeree have any duty to communicate acceptance to the offeror?

Are there any standards for how an acceptance must be communicated?

When does acceptance become effective?

What is the "mailbox rule"?

What happens if an offeree attempts to accept after the offer is terminated?

What happens if an acceptance of an offer includes additional terms or conditions in the acceptance?

What is the Mirror Image Rule?

What is the rule for additional or different terms in the acceptance of an offer under the UCC?

What happens when the offer is accepted through an electronic system, such as an auction format?

Are there any special provisions for Terms on Packaging in Shrinkwrap?

When are terms printed on the top of packages enforceable?

What are "Clickwrap" contract provisions?

What constitutes a rejection of an offer?

CHAPTER 5: FORMING A CONTRACT: CONSIDERATION

What is consideration?

What constitutes a legal detriment?

Do gifts by one party constitute consideration?

Can past consideration (consideration from a prior agreement) serve as consideration for a contract?

What constitutes adequate consideration?

Are there any other special forms of consideration?

What is an illusory promise?

Are exclusive dealing agreements illusory in nature?

What if a contract states that consideration is rendered, but it is not?

Are any contracts enforceable without consideration?

CHAPTER 6: DEFENSES TO ENFORCING A CONTRACT

What is an enforceable and a valid contract?

What is a void contract?

What defenses make a contract void (rather than voidable)?

What is unconscionability?

What is procedural unconscionability?

What is substantive unconscionability?

What is a contract that is illegal or violates public policy?

What is mental incapacity and how does it affect contract enforceability?

How does mental incapacity affect a minor child's ability to contract?

How does mental impairment (such as illness) affect a contract?

What is duress and how does it affect contract enforceability?

What is undue influence and how does it affect contract enforceability?

When does a mistake by the parties affect contract enforceability?

What is a mutual mistake and how does it affect contract enforceability?

When will a unilateral mistake make a contract voidable?

Are there special situations where a mistake does not give rise to a defense?

What is misrepresentation and how does it affect contract enforceability?

How does duress or undue influence by a third party affect contract enforceability?

What remedies are available to parties to a void contract?

CHAPTER 7: CONTRACTS REQUIRED TO BE IN WRITING – THE STATUTE OF FRAUDS

Do all contracts have to be in writing to be enforceable?

What does the statute of frauds require?

What kinds of contract must be in writing under the statute of frauds?

What type of signature is required for contracts under the statute of frauds?

Are there any special signature requirements for merchants?

Can a contract be enforceable if it fails to satisfy the statute of frauds requirements?

What statute of frauds exceptions apply to contracts for the sale of goods of $500 or more?

What exceptions to the statute of frauds apply to contracts for the sale of real estate?

What exceptions to the statute of frauds apply to contracts with durations of more than 12 months?

What is promissory estoppel?

CHAPTER 8: CONTRACTS & THIRD PARTIES – RIGHTS & DUTIES

Do third parties have any right to enforcement a contract to which they are not parties?

What contractual rights does a donee beneficiary have?

What contractual rights does a creditor beneficiary have?

When can a third-party beneficiary prevent modification of a contract to which she is a beneficiary?

Can contracts be assigned to other parties?

What is required to assign a contract?

Are there contracts that cannot be assigned?

Can a contract be assigned to multiple parties?

Can an assignment be revoked?

Can a contract be modified after assignment?

Can a party delegate duties under a contract?

Is a delegator relieved of responsibility after delegating the contract?

Is the delegatee liable under the contract if no novation takes place?

CHAPTER 9: INTERPRETING CONTRACTUAL TERMS

What general principle(s) are used in interpreting contractual provisions?

Do courts employ any rules to aid the interpretation of contracts?

What is the significance of a prior course of performance, dealing, or trade usage in interpreting a contract?

What is course of performance and dealing?

What is trade usage and why is it important?

What is the parole evidence rule?

When does the parole evidence rule apply to a contract?

What is "integration" and why is this concept important to contract interpretation?

What is a complete integration and why does it matter?

What is partial integration and why does it matter?

How does the court determine if a writing is a partial or complete integration?

What is an integration clause and how does it relate to integration?

When does the parole evidence rule not bar the consideration of extrinsic evidence to a contract?

How can extrinsic evidence be used to clear up ambiguities?

What is a patent and latent ambiguity?

CHAPTER 10: MODIFYING A CONTRACT

When and how can a contract be modified?

Does a modification have to be supported by consideration?

Can parties waive the requirement that a modification be in writing?

Can an unenforceable attempt at modifying a contract waive the original contract terms?

CHAPTER 11: WARRANTIES

What is a warranty in a contract?

Do warranties apply to goods and services?

What constitutes an express warranty by the seller of a good?

What is the implied warranty of title for goods?

What is the implied warranty of merchantability for goods?

What is the implied warranty of fitness for a particular purpose for goods?

Can a seller disclaim the implied warranties?

What is a general disclaimer of warranties?

Can a general disclaimer of warranties disclaim an express warranty?

CHAPTER 12: PERFORMANCE OF THE CONTRACT

What is the duty of performance?

What does it mean to discharge one's duty of performance?

What is complete, partial, and substantial performance?

What are "conditions of performance" in a contract?

What is an express and implied condition?

What is a condition precedent and condition subsequent?

What are concurrent conditions?

What is fulfillment of a condition?

What is strict fulfillment of a condition?

What is substantial fulfillment of a condition?

Are there any excuses that make a contract enforceable when a condition is not fulfilled?

What standards apply if a contract makes approval by a third party an express condition in the contract?

What if a condition to a duty to perform is based upon one party's approval of a situation?

What events or conditions discharge a party's contractual duties to perform?

What is rescission of a contract?

What is an accord and satisfaction?

What is a substitute contract?

What is novation?

What is a release?

What is impossibility of performance?

What is impracticability?

What is supervening frustration of purpose?

CHAPTER 13: BREACH OF CONTRACT

What is breach of contract?

What is a material breach of a contract?

What are a party's rights to cure a material breach?

What does it mean to "tender performance"?

What is a non-conforming tender of goods?

What are the rights of a party to reject a non-conforming tender of goods?

What happens if there is a defective tender in a single shipment under an installment contract?

When are goods deemed accepted and, thus, rejecting the tender offer is not possible?

Can a party revoke the acceptance of goods?

What are a seller's rights to cure a non-conforming delivery or tender of goods?

What is anticipatory repudiation?

How does a party indicate that she is going to breach the contract and allow the other party the right of anticipatory repudiation?

What is a party's right to demand assurances of performance from another party?

What are the rights of a party who anticipatorily repudiates a contract?

Can a party who repudiates the contract undo or withdraw her repudiation?

What are the general defenses to a breach of contract?

CHAPTER 14: REMEDIES FOR BREACH OF CONTRACT

What are a seller's rights in the event of breach by a buyer?

What are the buyer's rights in the event of breach by a seller?

What remedies are available to a party for breach of contract?

What are compensatory damages?

What are expectation damages?

What are consequential damages?

What are liquidated damages?

What are nominal damages?

What are punitive damages?

What is restitution?

What is specific performance?

What is rescission?

What is reformation?

Does the non-breaching party have a duty to mitigate the amount of damages?

CHAPTER 1: INTRODUCTION TO CONTRACTS

Overview

Why is it important for entrepreneurs and managers to understand contracts?

The legal system within the United States is a primary contributor to the economic prosperity of the nation. Confidence in the ability to assert or enforce one's rights in an agreement or bargain is essential to promote trade or economic activity. The contract is the primary tool used to memorialize the relationship between individuals. The ability to enforce one's rights through legal channels depends almost entirely upon the nature of the contractual relationship.

This text provides easy-to-understand explanations of all of the important aspects of contract law. We use everyday examples commonly faced by small businesses and large corporations to put the rules into context. It is advisable to consult a competent legal professional when drafting a contract; nonetheless, understanding how to form a contract, interpret its provisions, determine the rights and obligations of the parties, and identify the consequences of failure to perform are important skills for any entrepreneur or manager.

What is a Contract?

In plain terms, a contract is a form of agreement. More specifically, it is an agreement that outlines the rights, duties or obligations of the parties to the agreement. Let's begin by looking at the contract in terms of promises between two parties. Promises between individuals form a contract when one party makes a promise to another party that she will do something (or forgo doing something) in exchange for the other party's promise to do something (or promise to forgo doing something). This is a "bilateral contract." Also, one party may promise to do something in exchange for the other party's actual performance of an activity demanded by the promisor. This is a "unilateral contract."

- *Example:*

    Party 1: *I will pay you $5 if you will wash my car.*

    Party 2: *Sure, that sounds good.*

- *Example:*

    Party 1: *I will pay you $500 if you do not paint your house that hideous orange color.*

    Party 2: *Sure, I won't paint my house.*

Both of these examples contain promises between the parties that are enforceable contracts. The first example illustrates a promise to do something; while the second example illustrates a promise to forgo doing something that the promisor has the ability or legal right to do. We will discuss this issue further in the following chapters. The important thing to remember is that a contract involves a promise by at least one party and rights and obligations of all parties to the agreement.

Do the parties to a contract have to understand the rules of contract?

You may have a number of misconceptions about what it takes to form a legally binding contract. It surprises many people to know that a contract does not always have to be in writing to be enforceable. In fact, the parties do not have to realize or understand that their agreement is indeed a contract. Despite the formalities in place or the intent of the parties, a contract arises in law pursuant to the words and activities of the parties to the agreement. As you will learn further in this text, what constitutes a contract varies with the subject matter and relationship between the parties to the agreement.

Some examples may help introduce you to the need to understand basic contract law principles.

- *Example:*

  Party 1: *I will pay you $5 if you will wash my car.*

  Party 2: *Sure, that sounds good.*

- *Example:*

  Party 1: *I will sell you my car for $5,000.*

  Party 2: *Sure, that sounds good.*

Both of these examples are oral contracts. In the first example, we likely have a legally enforceable contract. In the second example, the contract is likely not legally enforceable. While these examples seem very simple at first glance, there are many aspects of contract law implicated by these situations. At the end of this text you will be able to make a laundry list of considerations in determining whether each situation results in a legally enforceable contract and what are the obligations of the parties in each situation.

What exactly is contract law and from where does it originate?

Generally, state law governs the formation of contracts. In some cases, countries will ratify or adopt model laws governing contractual relationships. For purposes of this text, we will focus on the domestic laws governing contractual relationships in the U.S. State contract law comes in two forms, statutes and common law. Statutory law, as the name implies, is determined by statutes passed by a state's government. Common law, on the other hand, is the law that arises pursuant to judicial interpretation of a given situation or statute. Together these laws make up the body of contract law that applies within a given state's jurisdiction.

How is common law created?

Common law is the law created through judicial interpretation of statutory law or regulations. If a contract is challenged in court, the judge will instruct the jury on the statutory or prior case law in place that governs the contract. The jury will then apply this law in determining liability in the case at hand. When the court's decision goes up for appeal, the appellate court may review the law to determine whether it was applied correctly and whether the law is constitutional. The court's opinion provides precedent for how that court and any subordinate courts in that jurisdiction should apply the law going forward. This opinion is now part of the "common law."

How do legislators come up with statutory law?

State legislators create statutes that govern contractual relationships. These legislators draw on legal resources provided by third-party groups in drafting and interpreting laws. Perhaps the two most influential legal resources affecting the drafting of statutory contract law are the Restatement of Contracts and the Uniform Commercial Code. These two documents are model laws written by professional or governmental entities to guide legislators who draft state contract law. These model laws also influence judges who interpret contract law. Most states have adopted statutes that resemble or copy exactly these model laws. As such, you can study model laws to acquire a broad understanding of how contract law works. You can then look to the specific laws of your state to determine the exact law that applies to a given situation.

What is the Restatement of Contract?

The Restatement of Contracts (Restatement) is published by the American Law Institute. This group studies the trends in contract law development and drafts model provisions or statutes. The Restatement deals primarily with contracts that do nott involve the sale of goods. When learning the U.S. laws governing contracts concerning anything other than the sale of goods, you may refer to the Restatement provisions for guidance. While each state has its own contract law, it generally tracks closely the provisions of the Restatement. Remember, the Restatement is not binding; rather, it serves as a persuasive resource. It is a strong influence on the development of common law, as it influences judges in the application and interpretation of contract law.

What is the Article 2 of the Uniform Commercial Code?

The Uniform Commercial Code (UCC) is a model law published by the American Law Institute and the National Conference of Commissioners on Uniform State Laws. The UCC is perhaps the single most influential model law affecting contractual relations. It covers many areas of commercial law and attempts to add uniformity to state codes governing commercial activity. The UCC has been uniformly accepted by nearly every state in the United States. As such, there is little variation in this area of law between states. When learning the law applicable to the sale of goods, this text will refer generally to the UCC provisions. Article 2 of the UCC provides model contract provisions applicable to contracts for the sale of goods.

Article 2 of the UCC focuses on the sale of goods between individuals and merchants. A sale includes any transfer of ownership for a given price. The definition of goods includes any manufactured product, crops, timber, livestock, attachments to land, exchanged currencies, mined minerals, etc. Notably, the definition excludes items of intellectual property, securities, non-commodity currencies, and un-mined minerals. To be subject to the provision of the UCC, goods must be the primary purpose of the contract. If services are the primary purpose of the agreement, then the incidental inclusion of goods is not covered by the UCC or corresponding state statutes.

Why is there a distinction between individuals and merchants under the UCC?

The UCC contains numerous provisions that are unique or only apply to merchants. A merchant is an individual who deals in specialty goods or has special knowledge or skill regarding the goods involved in the transaction. Generally, any individual or business that carries consumer items and offers some level of knowledge or service with relation to those items is considered a merchant for purposes of the UCC. Merchants are subject to higher standards of care, good faith, and fair dealing than non-merchants. This provides greater rights for individuals entering into contracts with merchants.

- *Note*: An individual who sells a personal item would not be a merchant, even if she is very knowledgeable about the item.

CHAPTER 2: ANATOMY OF A CONTRACT

Introduction

What are the terms of a contract?

As previously discussed, many agreements are never reduced writing; rather, they exist only in the understandings and beliefs of the parties to the agreements. These oral contracts demonstrate the belief in a common understanding between the parties or trust that the other party will comply with that understanding, and a lack of awareness of the potential legal pitfalls that frequently befall oral contracts. Not surprisingly, parties to an oral contract may be unaware of the extent of the rights, obligations, and duties present in their oral contract. Despite these negatives, oral contracts are far more common than their written counterparts. As such, it is extremely important to understand what makes an oral agreement into an enforceable contract.

- *Note*: The following chapters are dedicated to explaining when an agreement becomes an enforceable contract, the terms of that contract, the rights and obligations associated with that contract, and the remedies available for failure to live up to those obligations.

What are the benefits of a written contract?

Unlike an oral contract, a written contract provides a great deal of certainty to the agreement between the parties. The written contract, at a minimum, will contain the necessary terms to make the contract enforceable. These basic terms provide the backdrop for any other terms that may be implied by law or inferred from the context of the relationship. In many ways the written provisions are limiting, as the parties are now limited in their ability to assert conflicting accounts of the rights and obligations under the agreement. While there may still be room for alternative interpretations of certain provisions, the written contract establishes a baseline understanding that governs the relationship between the parties.

- *Note*: There are numerous influences on the interpretation of a written contract. For example, the context of the agreement may allow for varied interpretations of the terms of the agreement. Contract law may make inferences or supply additional terms to fill the gaps left by the written terms of the contract. As such, it is important to understand the common organization of written contracts to address the primary issues of concern between parties.

Anatomy of a Written Contract

What are the major components of a written contract?

Written contracts vary in structure, terms, length, formality of language, etc. In many ways, the contract is the creative product of the drafter. She will include and arrange the provisions of the contract in the manner most appropriate to the agreement being memorialized. Nonetheless, common practice in drafting written contracts provides for categories of provisions and a general structure for those provisions. The main categories and organization of common written contract provisions are as follow:

- Preamble, Recital, Words of Agreement
- Definitions
- Action Section (Consideration)
- Reps & Warranties
- Covenants & Rights
- Conditions to Obligations
- Endgame Provisions & Remedies
- General Provisions
- Signatures

Each of these provisions serves a specific function in allocating the rights and duties of the parties to the agreement. Written contracts will contain any combination of or all of these provisions and no two contracts will look exactly the same. Understanding the purpose or function of these provisions facilitates one's comfort and proficiency in reading, understanding, negotiating, and drafting a contract.

What is the preamble to a written contract?

The preamble states the name of the agreement, its date of execution, and the parties involved. If the parties are businesses, then the preamble will identify the type of entity and the state of organization. The preamble provides a descriptive noun, such as "Buyer" and "Seller," used to refer to the parties throughout the rest of the document.

- *Example*: This Sales Agreement ("Agreement") is made as of September 18, 2009 (the "Effective Date") between John Smith, an individual with an address at 123 Peachtree St., Atlanta, Georgia ("Buyer"), and Goizueta, Inc., a corporation organized pursuant to section 123-345 of the Annotated Code of Georgia, with an address at 456 University Lane, Decatur, Georgia ("Seller").

What are the recitals?

Recitals are an optional part of a written contract. Their purpose is to provide background information relevant to the agreement. They often state the parties' general understanding of the situation and their purpose or intent in entering into the agreement. This section does not contain or create any duties, rights, or obligations in the contract, as nothing in the recitals is enforceable.

- *Example*:

    A. WHEREAS, Seller is a supplier of parts for _____.

    B. WHEREAS, Buyer is currently a member of _____.

- *Note*: Parties should take care not to include any contract representations, covenants, or conditions in the recitals. The recitals can be very valuable for contract interpretation, however. Parties should consider including terms that provide for the intent of the parties or that recite the prior course of dealing or performance between the parties.

What are the words of agreement?

As explained in previous chapters, a contract requires an exchange of promises or a promise demanding immediate action. The words of agreement indicate the parties' intention to manifest their agreement to the promises and other terms contained in the contract.

- *Example:* **NOW, THEREFORE**, in consideration of the promises and the mutual covenants set forth herein and for other good and valuable consideration, the receipt and sufficiency of which are hereby acknowledged, the parties hereto covenant and agree as follows.

- *Example:* **NOW THEREFORE**, the Parties agree as follows:

What are the definitions and why are they included?

The definitions section allows parties to provide precise explanations of important contract terms. It can be used to introduce and explain trade terms or give special meaning to words that are susceptible of alternative meanings. It is also an important structural component of the written contract. A term that is defined in the definition section does not have to be repeatedly defined within the body of the contract. The initial definition in the section of defined terms is applicable to all uses of the term throughout the contract.

- *Example*: A sample definition within the definition section of a contract may appear as follows:

    1. "Security" - is defined as, any note, stock, treasury stock, security future, security-based swap, bond, debenture, evidence of indebtedness, certificate of interest or participation in any profit-sharing agreement, collateral-trust certificate, pre-organization certificate or subscription, transferable share, investment contract, voting-trust certificate, certificate of deposit for a security, fractional undivided interest in oil, gas, or other mineral rights, any put, call, straddle, option, or privilege on any security, certificate of deposit, or group or index of securities (including any interest therein or based on the value thereof), or any put, call, straddle, option, or privilege entered into on a national securities exchange relating to foreign currency, or, in general, any interest or instrument commonly known as a "security", or any certificate of interest or participation in, temporary or interim certificate for, receipt for, guarantee of, or warrant or right to subscribe to or purchase, any of the foregoing.

- *Note*: Many written contracts fail to include a section dedicated to defining key terms.

Without the defined terms section, parties must define terms within the body of the written contract. This can make the contract long and cumbersome to read. Also, it increases the likelihood of dispute if the definition is not applied uniformly in all sections of the contract. Likewise, the failure to define a term anywhere in the contract may lead to disputes as to the intended meaning of the term.

What is the action section?

This section contains the exchange of promises that is the subject matter of the agreement. It will specifically identify the value to be exchanged between the parties. For example, it will identify goods or services to be provided to the other party. It will also indicate the total amount and unit rate of currency exchanged in the transaction. This section sets the stage for all of the other contractual provisions that support this exchange of value.

- *Example*: "At Closing, Seller shall deliver to Buyer a mint-condition, baseball card depicting Mickey Mantle and produced by Topps Baseball, Inc., in 1952 (hereinafter "Baseball Card")."

- *Example*: "At Closing, Buyer shall deliver to Seller a certified check in the amount of $20,000 U.S. dollars."

- *Note*: There may be multiple actions required of either or both parties to the transaction that are incidental to the exchange of value that is the subject of the agreement. Some of these requirements may be outlined in the covenants section of the contract.

What are representations and warranties?

Representations are assurances by a party that certain facts or circumstances surrounding the contract are true. Oftentimes the reason for the parties entering into the contract depends entirely upon these facts or circumstances being true. Warranties are assurances by a party that certain representations are true or will be true at the consummation of the transaction. The representations and warranties allow the party receiving the assurances a cause of action for misrepresentation against the other party in the event the representations or warranties are not true or accurate.

- *Example*: "Seller represents that he is the sole owner and interest holder of Baseball Card."

- *Example*: "Seller warrants that at the time of closing he will remain the sole owner and interest holder of Baseball Card."

What are covenants?

Covenants are ancillary promises by the parties to undertake some action or cause some action to be taken prior to the consummation of the agreement. These promises involve incidental activities by either party necessary to bring about the circumstances or value intended by the contract. These provisions provide parties with protection against a failure by the other party to complete the ancillary activities necessary to carry out the purpose of the contract.

- *Example*: "Seller shall continue to maintain the Equipment in accordance with industry standards until Closing."

- *Note*: Covenants should only cover activities within the control of the parties. Any important actions required of third parties should be placed in the conditions section.

What are conditions?

Conditions are situations that must arise or facts that must be true before one or both parties have the obligation to perform their obligations under the contract. The conditions can regard the physical state of the subject matter of the contract, the completion of a covenant by the other party, or completion of all required actions by a third party.

- *Example*: "Seller must have a licensed mechanic of Buyer's choosing to inspect and provide a written opinion as to the functionality of the Equipment prior to Closing."

- *Note*: Conditions are extremely important to understand for both parties. They can excuse any or all obligations under the contract, and they are generally the strongest protections afforded the parties.

What are the endgame provisions?

Endgame provisions provide consequences for a failure of a representation, warranty, condition, covenant, or an obligation in the action section of the agreement. Further, they may adjust the duties and obligations pursuant to a misrepresentation, violation of law, supervening force, death, bankruptcy, or the occurrence of any other special event. They may also contain remedies available to the parties in the event of any such occurrence.

- *Example*: "If a majority of corporate directors vote to approve the dissolution of the company, all options to purchase preferred shares immediately vest in Buyer."

- *Note*: It is impossible to list all of the possible combinations of situations that the endgame provisions may cover. These provisions will be closely tailored to the type of contract and specific risks inherent therein.

What are the general provisions?

General provisions are generally referred to as boilerplate. These provisions regard the governance or management of the contract. Examples of boilerplate provisions include:

- The choice of law governing the agreement,

- The forum and legal jurisdiction in the event of contract dispute,

- How and where notice to any party should be delivered,
- The integrations clause,
- Amendments,
- Assignments and delegations,
- Successors and assigns
- Severability
- Merger and integration clause.

What is the signature block?

The final part of most written contracts consists of the statement of authority and the signature blocks. As discussed earlier in the text, the contract must be signed by someone with authority to enter into the agreement.

- *Example*:

"In Witness Whereof, the parties hereto agree to the terms and provisions contained herein."

ABC, Inc. _____(Signature)
        John Doe, President

Dated: _____

CHAPTER 3: FORMING A CONTRACT – THE OFFER

Overview

Contracts may arise either through the intentions of the parties, through their actions, or as a result of law or equity (fairness). We begin our discussion of contract formation by talking about express and implied contracts.

What is an express contract?

These are contracts formed through the discussion or negotiation of the parties. Generally, the parties intend to form a contract and openly discuss or negotiate its terms.

- *Example:* Tom says to Eric, "I will sell bricks to you in lots of 5,000 bricks (a cube) at $.89 per brick." Eric replies, "Excellent! I will purchase 10 cubes for my upcoming construction project." The parties then write down these statements on a napkin and sign it. In this case, the parties have formed an express, written contract. The contract is "express" because the parties stated specific terms of an intended agreement. It does not matter that the contract lacks formality. As previously stated, however, parties do not necessarily have to intend or even realize that they have entered into a contract. One such scenario is an implied-in-fact contract.

- *Note*: While an express contract does not necessarily have to be in writing, failing to write out a contract for the sale of goods may affect its enforceability. This issue is discussed in greater detail in later chapters.

What is an implied-in-fact contract?

This type of contract arises from the conduct of the parties, rather than from their intention to form an agreement. In the absence of an express agreement, the parties carry on some type of activity that is sufficient to considered a contractual relationship under the law. Restated, the facts of the situation (the actions of the individuals) make it reasonable for a court to determine that a contract exists under the applicable law. Some of the necessary elements to establish an enforceable contract may be missing (discussed later); but the activities of the parties, nonetheless, fill in or supply the missing elements.

- *Example*: John asks his accountant, Sarah, for professional advice. John knows that Sarah is a CPA and charges clients for her professional advice. Even if there is no mention of charges or a willingness to pay for advice, John's actions imply a promise to pay for any advice provided by Sarah. John will likely be responsible for paying a reasonable rate for Sarah's advice, even though he did not make an express promise to pay her. Further, John may not have intended to form a contract, but the facts of the situation are sufficient for a court to find that a contract was formed under the applicable law.

In some cases the parties' actions do not demonstrate an understanding by each party that a contract exists. That is, their activity does not demonstrate the elements of an enforceable contract. In such situations, the law may determine that an implied-in-law contract exists.

What is an Implied-in-Law or Quasi-Contract?

An implied in law or quasi-contract is a contract formed by judicial order to promote fairness among the parties. In these types of contracts, the necessary elements of the contract are absent. The court decides to step in and impose obligations on the parties as if an express contract exists.

A common scenario in which an implied-in-law contract arises is through unjust enrichment. When one party is unfairly benefited ("unjustly enriched") at the expense of another, the law may imply a duty on the first party to pay the second even though there is not contract between the two parties.

- *Example*: John rents land to Tom and, during the rental period, with the understanding that he will sell Tom the land to build his home. Tom begins the process of clearing the land and preparing it to build a home. After Tom has the ground leveled for the foundation, John decides to go back on his promise. As you will learn later, this agreement is not a valid, enforceable contract because there is no consideration and it is not in writing. The court, however, determines that Tom justifiably relied on Tom's promise to sell the land. He further, undertook effort (and spent money) in reliance on that promise. To deny that an enforceable contract exists would prejudice Tom in a number of ways. The court, therefore, holds that there is an implied-in-law contract and John must sell the land to Tom.

- *Note*: If Tom makes a payment and accepts possession of the land, it may provide an exception to the writing requirement and make the contract enforceable.

Now that you understand the different ways in which a contract may arise, let's focus our attention on the elements necessary to form a valid contract.

Elements of a Contract

A contract requires that parties come to some form of agreement. While the extent of the agreement may vary, the key element is that each party express her agreement or mutual assent to some or all of the proposed terms. In determining whether the parties have reached an agreement, a court will use an objective standard. That is, would a reasonable person in the situation of each party understand that she has entered into an agreement? The court will also weigh the subjective intent of each party to the proposed agreement.

The basic building blocks of a contract include:

    1) offer by one party,

2) acceptance by another party, and

3) the presence of consideration (something of value) as the subject of the agreement.

Sometimes, an offer and an acceptance are collectively referred to as "mutual assent" of the parties to the agreement. Below we examine each element of a contract independently.

The Offer

What is an offer?

An offer is one party's promise and demand of another party. The offer must demonstrate an intent to provide the other party with the ability to accept the offer and form a valid contract.

- *Example*: "Winston, I will sell you my car for $10,000." This is a valid offer, as it contains a promise to transfer ownership of a specific item (the car) and there is a specific demand (pay to me $10,000). The party who can accept the offer is properly identified as Winston. There would likely not be a contract if I were to say, "Winston, I will sell you my car for the right price." Further, there would not be a contract if I openly stated in conversation that, "I would sell my car for $10,000." This broad statement may be an invitation for people to submit offers to buy the vehicle, but is likely not sufficiently definite to constitute a demand of another party.

- *Note*: The above example incorporates numerous elements that make up a valid offer. Each of these elements is discussed in greater detail below.

When is a communication or promise by one party not an offer?

There are numerous types of communication between parties that are not promises, do not contain demands, and do not manifest the intent necessary to bind oneself in an agreement. Examples of non-offers include:

- statements of opinion,

    - *Example*: "I can easily sell this business for $250,000." This is not an offer to sell, but statement of opinion about the value of the business if it were for sale.

- statements of intent that do not invite acceptance,

    - *Example*: "At the end of the year, I am going to put my business on the market for sale for $250,000." This statement of future intention lacks the immediate intent to make an offer.

- invitations to others to make offers (such as advertisements in catalogs),

    - *Example*: Mark advertises in a local magazine that his products are for sale for

$39.99. Courts have interpreted these types of advertisements in magazines to be sufficiently indefinite in identifying an offeree to not constitute an offer. Rather, courts have held that magazine advertisements are requests to the population to submit offers for purchase. This is why a vendor can respond to a purchase order stating that the item is "sold out" or "no longer available."

- estimates of prices quoted as such, and

    - *Example*: Clark seeks advice from a local contractor about the cost for remodeling his office. The contractor inspects the premises and states, "Remodeling this building to your specifications will costs between $100,000 - 150,000."

- auctions that maintain reserve prices.

    - *Example*: Erik attempts to purchase a piece of equipment listed for sale on Ebay.com. At the end of the auction, he is the highest bidder. The auction, however, indicated that a minimum reserve price was set for the item. As such, Erik does not have a contract. His offer to purchase the item at a given price did not meet the seller's reserve price.

- *Example*:

    Party 1: I'm going to sell this car at the end of the year, if I can get $10,000 for it.

    Party 2: Done. I will pay you $10,000 for the vehicle.

In this case you do not have a contract. The original statement by Party 1 is not an offer that invites acceptance from the offeree. Party 1 is simply speaking generally of future intentions.

Who can be an offeror?

The offeror is the person making the offer. That person must intend and be able to make a commitment to the offeree. Intent is a mental aspect that requires that the offeror understand that she is making an offer. The ability of the offeror to make an offer means that the offeror must have the physical, mental, or otherwise legal ability to make the offer.

- *Example*: "I hate this stupid computer. I paid $400 for it, but I swear I would sell this thing for $50 right now." This is likely not an offer. First of all, this is an emotional statement made to demonstrate frustration. There is not specific intent behind the statement to actually make an offer to an identifiable offeree. If, on the other hand, an individual states, "Clara, I don't want this computer anymore. I paid $400 for it, but I will sell it to you for $300." This comment demonstrates a specific intent to sell the item and it communicates sufficient information that an identifiable offeree (Clara) to accept the offer.

- *Note*: Legal ability brings up questions of job title; actual, apparent, and implied authority; and the law of agency. Businesses carry on business through the efforts of their employees. Each employee has some level of authority (whether express or implied) to act on behalf of the business. Businesses often dispute the authority granted to agents purportedly acting on its behalf.

How specific must the offer be?

Generally, an offer and any resulting contract must be sufficiently specific to determine whether there is a breach of the obligation and what would be an appropriate remedy for the breach. The required specificity in the contract depends upon whether the contract falls under common law or is for the sale of goods.

Under the common law, contractual terms must be sufficiently definite and certain for an individual to accept the offer. This generally means that the offer must contain a description of the service or property and a price.

- *Example*: You cannot simply say, "I will purchase your land at a reasonable price." You must identify the piece of land you are offering to purchase and a price that you are offering for the land.

Under the UCC, the requirement to form an offer is a little different. Contracts for the sale of goods can leave open non-quantity terms to be decided at a future time. The contract will still be enforceable (i.e., is sufficiently definite) when certain terms are left open for the parties to determine and there is a "reasonable basis" for determining those terms. For example, the parties may leave open the price of the good, and a reasonable price under the circumstance will be imputed. Further, even a quantity of goods can be left open if the quantity to be purchased or sold is the total amount produced by the seller or the total amount needed by the buyer. These are known as "supply" and "exclusive dealing" contracts.

- *Example*: Terrence has a new business that involves printing and he needs to arrange for paper supplies. He makes the following offer to a local paper supplier (PaperSupply, Co.), "I will purchase all of the paper I need from PaperSupply, Co., at the same rate that you currently charge to Printers, Inc., for paper supplies." Printer's, Inc., is another company in town that Terrence knows purchases paper from PaperSupply Co. While this offer leaves open the price, the contract it is a valid offer because there is a reasonable basis for determining the applicable price. Also, the offer does not fail for indefiniteness simply because it does not state a specific amount. Stating that Terrence is bound to purchase all of the paper he needs is likely sufficient to constitute an exclusive dealing contract. Terrence is bound to purchase only from PaperSupply Co., for all of his paper needs.

- *Note*: Most advertisements, catalogs, and web page price quotes are considered too indefinite to form the basis for a contract, unless they are specific about the quantity of goods being offered, as well as the intended offeree.

Understanding Contracts for Entrepreneurs & Managers

When does the offer go into effect?

At common law, an offer generally becomes effective when a person empowered to accept the offer (an offeree) receives it. This is important, as there is often more than one offeree to a particular offer.

- *Example*: Ralph is a construction contractor who is soliciting offers from sub-contractors to paint a house that he is building. Tim, a subcontractor in the area, sends in a written offer to paint the house for $5,000. Ralph is empowered to accept the offer the minute he receives it in the mail. At the same time, Tim makes an offer to paint another house for Mitch, a different contractor. Tim sends this offer by email and it arrives to Mitch before the written offer arrives to Ralph. If Mitch accepts Tim's offer before Tim's offer to Ralph arrives, then Tim may revoke his offer before Ralph receives and is empowered to accept it. This example raises the issue of, when does an offeror have the ability to revoke an offer? The power to revoke an offer is discussed further below.

- *Note*: In today's business world, contracts are routinely formed *via* electronic communication. In contracts for the sale of goods, the UCC provides that an offer is generally effective upon receipt by an offeree's electronic communication system. That is, the offer is effective as soon as it appears in the offeree's email.

Once an offer is made, how long does it last?

An offer, unless it has a stated time period or is validly revoked, is presumed to remain open for a reasonable amount of time after it is made. The "reasonable" standard of time changes with respect to the situation, type of contract, relationship of the parties, and context of the offer. For example, an offer to purchase ripe vegetables will expire more quickly than an offer to sell a piece of furniture. As noted, if an offer states a specific time for acceptance, then the offer closes upon the expiration of that time.

- *Example*: Derek offers to sell Amber a single piece of equipment at a stated price. He writes all of the information down in the offer and mails it to her. Amber receives the offer the next day. She thinks about the offer for a couple of days and then replies to Derek in writing that she will accept the offer. This likely gives rise to a valid contract. The offer was silent about the time period to accept the contract. Responding within a couple of days is likely a reasonable period. Derek did not revoke the offer prior to Amber's acceptance, so there is likely a valid contract. If, however, Amber had waited one month to reply to Derek's offer, this is likely not a reasonable period of time. If Derek has already sold the equipment or simply no longer wishes to sell the piece of equipment to Amber, he would have a valid argument that the offer is no longer valid and that there is no contract.

- *Note*: If an offer is time specific, the time for accepting an offer begins to run as soon as it is (or should be) received. This is true even when there is a delay in delivery or a failure to check one's mail. Thus, the offer could expire before it is actually received by the offeree. There also may be a presumption of when an offer expires, based upon the context of the transmission of the offer. For example, an offer made in-person or over the telephone may be presumed to expire at the end of the conversation, unless there is a clear intent to leave it open.

So, by what means can an offer close or be terminated?

If an offer terminates, it can no longer be accepted. The offer automatically closes under a number of situations, including:

- a specific provision in the offer;

    - *Example*: Zora offers to sell equipment to Mindy to use in her business. The offer specifically states that Mindy must accept the offer by sending a down payment to Zora by the end of the week. If Mindy fails to make the down payment as demanded by the offer, the offer expires and Mindy cannot later accept the offer.

- after a reasonable amount of time;

    - *Example*: Zora offers to sell equipment to Mindy to use in her business. The offer does not contain any specific time period for accepting the offer. Mindy will have a reasonable time to accept the offer. A reasonable time is determined by the context and subject matter of the offer. What is the nature of the business? What type of equipment is it? Will delaying the sale of the equipment detriment Zora (such as having to pay storage fees)?

- upon rejection by the offeree;

    - *Example*: If Mindy rejects the offer from Zora, she cannot later come back and accept that offer. The offer terminates the moment her rejection of the offer is communicated to Zora. Mindy may now make an offer to Zora to purchase the equipment, but that puts the power of acceptance in Zora's hands.

- by the offeree making a counter-offer;

    - *Example*: In the case of Mindy and Zora, if Mindy states that she will purchase the equipment, but at 50% lesser prices, this is a rejection and counter-offer to Zora.

- by the offeror's express revocation (prior to acceptance);

    - *Example*: If Zora withdraws the offer before Mindy is able to accept it, the offer is revoked and cannot be accepted.

- the subject-matter of the offer no longer exists or is destroyed;

- *Example*: If the he specific piece of equipment that Zora intends to sell to Mindy is destroyed, then the object of the contract is gone. As such, the offer to sell that piece of equipment terminates.

- the offeror loses mental capacity or passes away; or

    - *Example*: If Zora gets into an accident that causes her to lose capacity or is terminally injured, her offer to sell the equipment expires.

- the subject-matter of the offer becomes illegal.

    - *Example*: The equipment that Zora offers to sell Mindy becomes illegal because of environmental regulations; therefore, the offer terminates and cannot then be accepted my Mindy.

As noted above, revoking the offer prior to acceptance by the offeree terminates the offer.

How do you revoke an offer?

Revocation must come from the offeror or his agent before the offeree accepts the offer. The revocation must be clear and unequivocal. The offer is also revoked if the offeree learns of activity by the offeror that demonstrates that the offer is no longer open. A reasonable person standard is used in each of these determinations.

- *Example*: Alice offers to sell her car to Mary at a given price. Mary does not immediately accept the offer. A week later, Mary learns that Alice sold the car to Jim. Learning of Alice's actions, which is inconsistent with her offer to Mary, is sufficient to revoke Alice's offer.

- Note: The "reasonable person" standard is an objective standard that determines how a reasonable person would act in a specific situation or context.

Can all offers by revoked?

There are some special circumstances or types of offers that cannot be revoked. The most common types of irrevocable offers are:

- valid options contracts that are supported by consideration (value);

    - *Example*: Sara works for Big Corp. Big Corp grants options to Sara to purchase stock in the corporation at a given price. The option contract is a form of offer, as it allows Sara to purchase stock if she so desires. She is not obligated to act. Since the option is the subject of a contract supported by consideration (Sara provides services in exchange for the option) it cannot be revoked.

- the offer and activity of the offeree give rise to an implied-in-law contract;

- *Example*: Gail is a marketer who agrees to help Hank's startup business to grow. Hank does not have the money to pay Gail; but, in exchange for her services, he agrees to compensate her by awarding her a certain number of shares of the business. Hank includes a contingency that, he will only transfer equity to Gail if the business achieves a specific level of profits at the end of the year. The business performs very well as a result of Gail's marketing efforts. At the end of the year, Hank decides to make a major purchase that drastically reduces the business' reportable profits. Hank refuses to transfer any equity in the company to Gail because the company technically did not reach its profit target. Gail sues Hank. While there is technically no breach of contract, the court may imply the obligation upon Hank to pay her the reasonable value of her services.

- *Note*: Generally, an implied in law contract arises when the court uses its power of equity to make the outcome of a situation fair and just. A common use of the equitable power to declare an implied-in-law contract is when there is foreseeable, detrimental reliance by the offeree on the offeror's promise.

• in a unilateral contract, the offeree begins performance (mere preparation is likely insufficient), but has not yet completed her obligations;

- *Example*: Amy offers to pay Zeke $500 to build an ADA compliant ramp into her business. As part of the offer, Amy tells Zeek that he must begin building the ramp before the end of the week. Once Zeke begins to build the deck, he has to complete the job. Amy cannot revoke the contract during this period.

- *Note*: A unilateral contract is one where the offeror requires that the offeree accept the contract by undertaking performance. That is, the offeror requires action rather than a return promise to perform from the offeree. In a unilateral contract without a specific time for performance, the offeror must give an offeree who has begun performance a reasonable amount of time to complete performance.

• a UCC merchant makes a firm offer (a written, signed offer that assures the offer will remain open) to buy or sell goods – even if the offer is not supported by consideration.

- *Example*: David is a merchant selling bicycles. He offers to sell a fleet of bicycles to the local school as part of a environmentally friendly commuting effort. The school's ability to purchase the bicycles is contingent upon the school receiving a highly anticipated grant. To accommodate this situation, David makes a signed, written offer that says it will remain open for 90 days. In this situation, David cannot withdraw the offer because it constitutes a "firm offer" by a merchant.

- *Note*: As demonstrated in the above example, a firm offer from a merchant states a specific time that it will stay open. The offer is enforceable and must remain open for that period of time, despite the absence of consideration. If the time period is not specifically stated, it must remain open for a reasonable amount of time. In no event will the time exceed three months.

When is the revocation effective?

Revocations are effective whenever the offeror provides notice of revocation to the offeree. That is, revocation is effective upon receipt.

- *Example*: Fanny agrees to install a new lightening system in Sam's recording studio for $10,000. Before Sam accepts the offer, Fanny realizes that she miscalculated the cost of the lighting system. She quickly revokes the contract by calling and notifying Sam. When Sam receives the call, he is preparing to sign and return the contract. Unfortunately for Sam, the revocation is effective when received and Sam cannot accept the contract.

- *Note:* Some courts have treated the revocation of an offer similarly to acceptance. This interpretation makes a revocation effective when it is sent, rather than when received.

Are the rules of offer and acceptance the same when dealing with automated ordering and fulfillment systems?

Contracting *via* an automated system is a new development in contract law. The UCC proposes that electronic contracting agents be treated similarly to principal parties to the contract. As such, the court would apply the above-discussed rules to the situation. The electronic system is merely an agent that possesses the authority to bind the principal.

CHAPTER 4: FORMING A CONTRACT – THE ACCEPTANCE

How do you accept an offer?

The offeree can accept the offer by any means reasonable under the circumstances. In any event, acceptance of the offer requires an unequivocal response demonstrating a willingness to accept the terms or conditions of the offeror's promise. The method of providing this unequivocal response varies between unilateral and bilateral contracts.

- *Example*: Hank sends a letter to Juliet offering to sell her a specific piece of equipment for $250. He does not indicate the method for acceptance of the offer. Hank receives a text from Juliet stating, "I accept your offer and I will buy the equipment at the stated price." This text message is sufficient to accept the contract. Given the circumstances, texting notice of acceptance to Hank is reasonable.

What is a bilateral and unilateral contract and how does it affect acceptance?

In previous chapters, we explained that a contract is an agreement that involves the exchange of promises between individuals. This is known as a bilateral contract. A bilateral contract requires that the offeree make an unequivocal return promise that acknowledges acceptance of offeror's promise. The offeree makes a promise to perform or carry out the offeror's demand at some point in the future. Failure to do so constitutes a breach of contract.

- *Example*: "I promise to pay you five dollars, if you promise to baby sit on Friday." If the offeree accepts, this is a bilateral contract, as it consists of mutual exchange of promises between individuals. It is not necessary to use the word promise. You simply have to express that you will perform the required action (sell the item or provide the service) at some point in the future.

- *Note*: In some cases, the offeree may attempt to accept the contract by simply beginning to perform the activity that is demanded by the offeror. In this case, while if the contract requires that an offeree accept by making a promise to perform, the contract may still be enforceable. If the offeree commences work and the offeror recognizes the activity and does nothing to stop it, the contract will likely be implied from the actions of the parties. The offer to form a bilateral contract becomes enforceable as a unilateral contract.

The second form of contract is known as a "unilateral contract." An offer to form a unilateral contract makes a promise in exchange for performance of the offeror's demand. A party must complete performance in order to accept the offer. Failure to complete performance by the offeree is not a breach, as no contract has been formed until performance is completed.

- *Example*: "I promise to pay you five dollars when you wash my car." In this case, one party promises to pay money in exchange for the activity of another person. She does not want a promise from the other party – she wants action. In turn, there is no contract until the other party actually washes the car.

- *Example*: Another example of this situation would be the promise to pay a bonus. Your boss says, "I promise to pay you a bonus if you reach your sales goal." In this case, you have a unilateral promise to pay in exchange for the other party carrying on an activity. There is no obligation for the boss to perform (pay money) until the employee completes the action (reaches the sales goal).

Can an offeror revoke a unilateral offer after the offeree begins performance, but has not completed?

No. Once the offeree begins performance, the offeree must allow her a reasonable amount of time to complete performance. Again, if the offeree does not fully perform, there is no acceptance of the offer.

- *Example*: Terry offers Arlene $500 if she will design a website for his new business. Arlene begins doing mockups of the website on her computer and sends a sample to Terry. Upon receiving the mockups, Terry decides to save money and use one of the pre-made website services to create the website. In this situation, Arlene has started performance and thereby accepted the offer. As such, Arlene has a reasonable time to accept the contract by completing performance.

- *Note*: There are generally exceptions to this rule. For example, the offeror may be able to revoke if the offeree's performance sufficiently deviates from a reasonable standard of acceptance. Further, if the offeree undertakes activity not reasonably related to the required services, the offeror can revoke the offer.

- *Note*: As previously noted, if an offeree fails to fully perform, then she may still be entitled to receive from the offeror the reasonable value of the services that she provided. This makes certain that the offeror does not receive a benefit without paying anything for the partially performed services. In this situation, the court may use its equity power to ensure a fair and just result. All courts have powers of equity.

What if the offeree does not respond to the offer?

Under the common law, the general rule is that silence by the offeree is not acceptance of an offer. There are, however, exceptions to this rule. If the relationship between the parties is such that it is not expected that the offeree reply, then silence by the offeree may constitute acceptance. Another example would be where the offeree readily understands that silence or a failure to respond means acceptance of the offer. This generally only arises in situations where the offeror and offeree have a history of prior dealings.

- *Example*: Tim tells Virginia that he will sell her ten bags of apples for $10 per bag and that she must reject the offer within 3 days. This is not a contract, as silence or failing to reject an offer is not acceptance. If, however, Tim regularly sells apples to Virginia on a recurring schedule and there is an understanding that Virginia will accept all shipments that are not rejected within 3 days of delivery, then failure to reject the delivery can constitute acceptance of the offer.

- *Note*: In the case of contracts between merchants under the UCC, silence may constitute acceptance of an offer. In some instances, a merchant is required to expressly reject goods that are delivered; otherwise, her silence constitutes acceptance of the contract.

What if an offeree does not respond to the offer but accepts deliver of the goods or services?

Under common law, if the offeree accepts goods or services with the knowledge that they are being offered or sold for a price, then there is a valid contract.

- *Example*: Mark walks into a dentist office and asks for a routine teeth cleaning. Upon beginning the cleaning, Mark is bound contractually to pay for the services he receives.

- *Note*: If the offeror does not agree to the offeree simply retaining the goods as acceptance of the offer (e.g., she expressly requires payment before there is acceptance), then she may still revoke the offer prior to the offeree accepting the goods.

After acceptance, can a failure to communicate acceptance to the offeror prejudice the offeree?

As discussed above, the offeree must generally communicate with the offeror to effect acceptance. If the offeree acts in a way that demonstrates acceptance, but fails to notify the offeror, the offeror may revoke the offer if she is somehow prejudiced by the offeree's silence.

- *Example*: Pete needs a logo for his new business immediately. He makes on offer to pay Alice to develop the logo. Alice begins working, but fails to notify Pete that she is working on the project. In the meantime, Pete, having not received a response from Alice, hires another designer to work on the logo. When Pete learns that Alice is working on the logo, he may be able to revoke the offer. He would be prejudiced if he had to pay for two designers. In this case, he may not have to pay for her services, as he did not receive any value from her beginning performance.

In a unilateral contract, does the offeree have any duty to communicate acceptance to the offeror?

Under the Restatement, the offeree in a unilateral contract simply has to perform in order to accept an offeror's offer.

- *Note*: If the offeree knows that the offeror has no way of knowing about his acceptance, the offeree must be diligent in notifying the offeror. Of course, this rule is not applicable if the offeror makes known that she does not need to be notified of acceptance.

- *Example*. Mary puts out an offer to a group of designers that she will pay $500 to anyone who designs a new logo for her website. Tom designs a really nice logo for her website. Tom should realize that Mary cannot know that he has accepted the contract by undertaking the design work. As such, Mary is not bound to the contract if Tom fails to notify her in a timely manner.

Under the UCC, the offeree must notify the offeror of her intent to accept by beginning performance within a reasonable time of the offer being made. If no, the offeror can treat the offer as having lapsed.

- *Example*: Alex makes an offer to pay Jude $10,000 for painting his cabin. Jude, without notifying Alex, begins painting the cabin approximately 2 months after the offer was made. Alex may be able to notify Jude that the offer was rejected and to stop painting the cabin. In such a case, there would not be a breach of contract, as the offer was not accepted within a reasonable time. Rather, Alex would simply owe Jude for the reasonable value of her painting services performed before she was notified to stop.

Are there any standards for how an acceptance must be communicated?

If the offer is not specific on the manner of acceptance, there is no mandatory method for communicating acceptance of an offer. Under the UCC, the offeree can employ any method that is reasonable under the circumstances. Under common law, the offeree may respond in the same manner as the offer or in any manner that is "customary in similar transactions at the time and place the offer is received."

When does acceptance become effective?

The offer may state the time when any acceptance becomes effective. Absent specific direction, an acceptance is effective as soon as it is sent or communicated by a reasonable means. If an improper method or means of communication is used, acceptance becomes effective as soon as it is received.

- *Note*: There is an exception to this general rule. If the offeree accepts by an unapproved method, the acceptance will be effective when sent if the offeror receives the acceptance within the prescribed time period allowed for acceptance by an approved method.

- *Example*: Mark offers to sell his land to Eric. Eric gives him notification of acceptance via mail, but the required method was hand-delivered letter. If Mark gave Eric until Friday to hand-deliver acceptance and Mark receives the mailed acceptance before Friday, then the method may be deemed effective at the time that Eric mailed it.

- *Note*: Special rules apply to other unique situations or types of agreement. For example, acceptance of an option contract is not effective until received by the offeror.

What is the "mailbox rule"?

Unless the offeror specifies a specific manner of acceptance, the offer is generally accepted when the offeree dispatches it (i.e., drops it in the mail or sends it with a courier). The importance of this rule is that the offeror cannot rescind the offer once the offeree has dropped it in the mail or placed it with a common carrier. Further, if an offer is made to multiple offerees, the first offeree to accept in any manner (including by dropping the acceptance in the mail) has a binding contract.

- *Example*: Whitney offers to sell her car to Victoria and Janice. She does not specify the manner of acceptance, but does require that Victoria or Janice accept the offer before Friday. Victoria drops her acceptance of the offer in the mail on Thursday at 1:00 P.M. Janice attempts to accept the offer in person at 2:30 P.M., that same day. Janice's acceptance is not effective, as Victoria as already accepted the contract. This is true even though Whitney has not yet received or is not aware of Victoria's acceptance.

- *Note*: The above example should demonstrate the offeror's peril in sending out offers to multiple individuals.

What happens if an offeree attempts to accept after the offer is terminated?

Generally, an offer is revoked if a valid acceptance is not communicated within the required time period.

- *Example*: Tom offers to paint Alex's house for $5,000, but Alex must accept the offer within 3 days. On the 4th day, Alex attempts to accept the offer. Tom is not bound in contract by Alex's late acceptance.

- *Example*: In the above example, Tom can waive the lateness of Alex's acceptance. This may give rise to a binding contract. Under the common law, the late acceptance is simply a new or counter-offer from Alex to Tom. Tom is therefore accepting Alex's offer.

- *Note*: The offeror can always waive the late notice and acknowledge the acceptance. If the offeror fails to respond or reject the late acceptance within a reasonable time, then it may result in a valid contract. As stated above, under the common law, the offeree's communication may be considered a counter-offer to the offeror.

What happens if an acceptance of an offer includes additional terms or conditions in the acceptance?

It depends on whether the contract is governed by common law or the UCC. Under the common law, the "Mirror Image Rule" applies. Under the UCC, the additional terms may be excluded from the contract.

What is the Mirror Image Rule?

The mirror image rule applies in common law contracts. It states that the terms of an acceptance of a contract must be exactly the same (or mirror) the terms of the offer. If the acceptance contains terms that are different from or add to the offer, then the acceptance is ineffective. Instead, the acceptance becomes a counter-offer to the offeror. Courts are split on whether minor, immaterial additions cause the acceptance to be defective. One theory is that these are mere suggestions to modify an already accepted agreement.

- *Example*: John offers to wash Will's car for $50. Will agrees, but says that John must also vacuum the interior. In this case, no contract is formed. Will effectively makes a counter-offer to John, stating that he will pay John $50 to wash and vacuum his car.

- *Note*: If the acceptance accepts mirrors the offeror's terms and merely suggests additional terms, the court may deem the acceptance sufficient.

What is the rule for additional or different terms in the acceptance of an offer under the UCC?

The UCC takes a different approach than the Restatement to additional or different terms in an acceptance. If the acceptance of the offer is unequivocal, then the UCC deems the acceptance effective. The effect of different or additional terms depends on whether the parties are merchants. If either party is not a merchant, then any additional or different terms are deemed suggestions for addition and do not become part of the contract. If both parties are merchants, the additional terms become a part of the contract unless: they materially alter the contract, acceptance is conditioned on the specific terms of the offer, or the offeror specifically rejects the additional or different terms.

- *Example*: Mary offers to sell a piece of equipment to Darla for $1,000. Darla accepts the offer by sending a check and a letter, but mentions that she would appreciate the ability to return the equipment within 30 days if anything is wrong with it. Neither Mary nor Darla is a merchant. If Darla did not expressly condition her purchase of the equipment on the acceptance of her proposal for the inclusion of a warranty, there is a binding contract and the warranty is not included.

- *Example*: In the above situation, if both parties are merchants, the warranty provision may be included in the contract. If a dispute arose, a court adjudicating the matter would determine whether the warranty provision materially altered the terms of the contract.

What happens when the offer is accepted through an electronic system, such as an auction format?

If the offeree has reason to know that she is accepting the contract *via* an electronic format, any additional terms that she may add within the electronic system do not become part of the contract.

- *Example*: You purchase an item at auction on an auction-style, website - such as Ebay.com. If you add additional terms to the purchase *via* the electronic system, those terms do not become part of the contract. The offer is contingent upon acceptance pursuant to the terms of the offer. The contract is complete at the time that you consummate the purchase.

Are there special provisions for requirements contracts and output contracts?

Yes. The UCC makes special provision for these types of contracts. In a requirements contract, the supplier agrees to supply all of the goods required by the buyer. Likewise, in an output contract, the purchaser agrees to purchase all of a supplier's output. The UCC deems requirements and output contracts valid, despite the absence of a specific number of items being purchased or sold. As such, the terms of the purchase (e.g., the amount or number purchased) may change with each order.

- *Example*: Denise enters into a contract with Idina to purchase all of the items of clothing that her company produces. This is an example of a output contract that is enforceable without specifically identifying the number of clothing items being purchase. In order to produce clothes Idina purchases fabric from Olivia. Olivia enters into a contract to supply all of the fabric that Idina requires. This is a supply contract that is enforceable despite the absence of a specific amount of fabric.

- *Note*: These agreements provide security to parties who are uncertain about the market supply or demand for a particular good. In these contracts, there is no fixed quantity of goods; rather, the quantity to be purchased or sold is determined by the needs of the buyer or production capability of the seller. In a requirements contract, the seller is generally not prohibited from selling to other buyers. In an output contract, the seller is generally restricted from selling to other buyers. The buyer, however, can buy from other sellers to meet its requirements.

Are there any special provisions for Terms on Packaging in Shrinkwrap?

Many consumer products are sold with the consumer's terms and conditions packaged or "shrinkwrapped" inside of the box. The consumer is unable to review these provisions and is often unaware that they exist until after the purchase is made. Some products (such a software) indicate that opening the shrinkwrap is deemed acceptance of these terms. Courts are divided on the enforceability of such provisions. Major cases on the subject involve the enforceability of warranty provisions and arbitration clauses.

- *Example*: Derek purchases a computer from Microtck. When the computer arrives, the terms of the purchase, including the limitations on the use of the software loaded on the computer, are inside of the box. The packaging indicates that opening the package and turning on the computer constitutes acceptance of the terms of sale. Courts are split as to whether these terms are enforceable. One theory posits that contract has been formed and opening the box and using the computer cannot unilaterally add previously undisclosed terms to the contract.

- *Note*: Merchants are advised to take care to disclose all terms at the time of purchase *via* pre-delivered documentation or disclosure provisions on the website.

When are terms printed on the top of packages enforceable?

The majority of courts hold that external terms printed on the top of a package prior to purchase are express terms of the agreement.

- *Example*: Harriet purchases a computer that has statement written on top of the box, "photo-editing software included." Upon opening the box, Harriet realizes that the disk supposedly containing the photo-editing software is missing. The store refuses to provide a replacement disk. This would be a breach of contract. The terms on the outside of the box are part of the bargain. Failing to include the photo-editing software is a breach of contract.

- *Note*: This general rule may change when the purchaser is unable to read these terms, such as when the item is purchased over the internet or there are other reasons preventing the general customer from reading or understanding the terms (e.g., a sticker is pasted over the written terms).

What are "Clickwrap" contract provisions?

Much of today's contracting takes place electronically. The terms of these transactions are included in boilerplate language within the website. Consumers are made to read (or scroll through) and click a button certifying that they have read and accept these terms. Most courts hold that these terms are binding upon the purchaser. Clicking the "I agree" button indicates express acceptance of the merchant's terms of sale.

- *Example*: Hannah purchases a new Apple computer from the Apple.com website. Before finalizing her purchase, she is asked to agree to the terms of sale, which are included in a long list of provisions. One of the provisions states, "you agree not to use I-Tunes to create a missile, or nuclear, chemical, or biological weapons." If Hannah accepts these terms, she is indeed contractually prohibited from using the I-Tunes software for any of these purposes.

- *Note*: A similar provision to the above example of a Clickwrap provision was actually included in Apple, Inc.'s, End-User License Agreement.

What constitutes a rejection of an offer?

Rejection of an offer is an unequivocal expression that the offer has been rejected. Unlike an acceptance (see Mailbox Rule), the rejection is not effective until received by the offeror.

- *Example:* Eric makes an offer to purchase supplies from Tom. Tom sends a rejection of the offer in the mail. Rethinking his position, Tom then calls Eric and accepts the offer. The acceptance is effective, as Eric has not yet received notice of the rejection of the offer.

CHAPTER 5: FORMING A CONTRACT – CONSIDERATION

What is consideration?

The definition of consideration is a bargained for exchange where each party incurs a legal detriment. In short, consideration means something of value. In any exchange of value, each party gives up their legal rights to something. Whether the parties cared about the thing given up or whether it had any monetary value is immaterial.

- *Example*: Nick enters into a contract with Agatha to complete the build-out construction in her new office. Agatha will pay Nick $5,000 for his work. In this situation, Nick is incurring a legal detriment (the duty to undertake work) and Agatha is incurring a legal detriment (paying $5,000). Both of these legal detriments constitute consideration.

- *Example*: "Tyson, I will pay you $100 if you sit silently and do not interrupt me for the rest of this presentation." If Tyson agrees and remains silent for the remainder of my presentation, then we have a valid contract. My $100 is valid consideration and Tyson forgoing his right to talk is valid consideration.

- *Note:* As demonstrated from the above examples, consideration can take any number of forms. The value does not actually have to be exchanged by the parties. It simply has to be the subject of a bargained for agreement between the parties.

What constitutes a legal detriment?

A legal detriment is undertaking an action for which there is no obligation or agreeing not to act when a person has the right to do so. In this sense, the loss of legal rights to the item or to do something is a detriment. In the context of a contract, the promise or action of each party is the inducement for the other party's promise or action. Either person's promise or action is consideration as it limits that person's rights not to perform the promise or action.

- *Example*: Think about a non-compete clause. One party promises money or benefits (such as a job) in exchange for another party agreeing not to compete with that party. The promise to not compete is consideration, because one party forgoes her right to carry on a trade (a legal detriment to her).

Do gifts by one party constitute consideration?

No. The legal detriment (relinquishing rights or ownership in the property) is only suffered by one party. So, promises by one party without some return promise or action constituting a legal detriment by the other party is not enforceable.

- *Example*: Susan says to Victor, "You can have my old laptop computer. I don't use it any more." The next day Susan's new computer is infected with a virus and stops working. She needs her old computer to continue her work while the new computer is being repaired. There is no valid contract transferring ownership of the computer to Victor, as there is no consideration from Victor to form a contract. As such, Susan may be able to reclaim the computer.

- *Note*: There are situations where the above example could constitute a valid contract or result in an implied-in-law contract. These situations are discussed below.

If one party provides a gift to another party and that gift is subject to specific conditions, this may constitute consideration. The agreement by the other party to adhere to those conditions is a legal detriment (i.e., the inability to use the gift in a given manner) can constitute consideration.

- *Example*: Melinda makes a gift to Bill of 5,000 acres of land. As part of the gift, Melinda requires that Bill use the land as a nature preserve. If Bill ever uses the land for anything other than a nature preserve, the gift is revoked and ownership reverts back to Melinda. In this situation, the gift is subject to a specific condition (use as a nature preserve). By accepting the gift, Bill is forgoing his right to use the property in any manner he so chooses. As such, the conditions on the gift constitute consideration and there is a binding contract. If Bill breaches the contract by using the land as a theme park, the remedy in the contract is for ownership to revert back to Melinda.

A gift from one party to another may be enforceable if some equitable rule (e.g., promissory estoppel) makes it enforceable as an implied-in-law contract.

- *Example*: In the example of Susan and Victor, suppose Victor decides to upload his very expensive software to the computer gifted from Susan. The software only allows for one download and cannot be transferred from one computer to another. Because Victor relies upon Susan's gift of the computer to his detriment (loss of his computer programs), then there may be an enforceable contract based upon promissory estoppel.

Can past consideration (consideration from a prior agreement) serve as consideration for a contract?

Generally, no. Prior consideration constituted a legal detriment at that time. If a person does not incur an additional legal detriment then there is no valid consideration.

- *Example*: Michelle hires Gloria to perform landscaping services in her yard. Michelle agrees to pay Gloria $1,000 for her services. Prior to beginning the job, Michelle tells Gloria that she has underpriced the project and it will cost $2,000. Michelle says, "I understand, I will pay you the $2,000 for the services." When Gloria completes the project, Michelle is not happy with the results. She does not believe the work is worth $2,000 and only pays Gloria $1,000. In this situation, there was a valid contract for $1,000. Gloria sought to adjust the contract without providing any new, additional consideration (i.e., she was going to perform the exact same services for a higher dollar amount). As such the contract modification likely will not be enforceable and Michelle will only have to pay Gloria $1,000.

- *Note*: An exception to this rule is when a party promises an additional legal detriment on top of an existing detriment. For example, I promise to pay a higher price if you deliver my goods more quickly than previously agreed. This is an additional legal detriment. On the other hand, a promise to pay a lesser amount than owed does not constitute consideration, unless it is involves an agreement to forgo a claim or dispute under the agreement (discussed below).

    - *Example*: If, in the above example, Gloria had added some additional services (or other value) to the new contract and Michelle accepted, this would have been new consideration and the new contract for $2,000 would have superseded the original $1,000 contract. Gloria could have agreed to complete the job more quickly, added a landscaping maintenance deal, etc. The additional consideration could be minimal.

- *Note*: Under the UCC, a preexisting obligation can form the consideration for a new contract. The only limitation to this rule is that a contract that is subject to the statute of frauds (i.e., must be in writing), any modification of that contract must also comply with the statute of fraud.

    - *Example*: Brad enters into a contract with Violet to sell her a piece of equipment for $1,000. Later, Brad discovers that he mis-priced the item. Violet agrees in writing to pay $1,200 for the equipment instead of the original $1,000. This agreement is enforceable even in the absence of new consideration. Remember, the new agreement must be in writing (comply with the statute of frauds) to be enforceable.

What constitutes adequate consideration?

Courts generally hold that any form of consideration is adequate. Courts do not judge the reasonableness of an exchange; rather, they simply determine whether there was some exchange of value.

- *Example*: Burt is purchasing a house from Ernie for $100,000. They enter into a purchase agreement, subject to a 15-day inspection period, where Burt can back out of the deal for any issues that arise during inspection. Burt inspects the property and finds some minor issues. Burt tells Ernie that he is only willing to pay $98,000 for the home in the current conditions. Burt agrees to the lower price. The parties execute an amendment modifying the original contract. The contract states that, "In exchange for $10, the parties agree to the following modifications to the previous contract ... ." The parties include this $10 language so that the modification to the contract is supported by consideration. The consideration is small or nominal in nature, but it is adequate to support the contract modification.

- *Note*: Some courts have held that "nominal consideration" that is given simply to create a binding contract may not be sufficient to make the contract enforceable.

Are there any other special forms of consideration?

Yes. Courts have recognized many unique situations that constitute valid consideration. For example, giving up one's right to contest or dispute a prior agreement can constitute consideration. Forgoing one's right to sue another person over a dispute or agreeing not to put forward a legally recognizable defense to a claim would also be valid consideration. This is a "release" or "waiver." Often, one party will offer a lesser payment than the amount owed in return for forgoing the right to further dispute the debt. If the other party accepts, then this promise constitutes valid consideration. We will see later, this situation is called an "accord and satisfaction."

- *Example*: Helen agrees to perform electrical work for Autumn for $1,000. Autumn is not happy with Helen's work and withholds payment. Helen threatens to sue Autumn for the payment. Autumn alleges breach of contract by Helen based on poor or incomplete performance. Rather than go to court, Autumn and Helen agree to settle the matter by Autumn paying Helen $800. In turn, Helen agrees forgo her right to sue Autumn for not paying $1,000. In this settlement, the parties both exchanged value by forgoing a right or entitlement.

- *Note*: In the above situation, there must be some uncertainty as to the merits of the dispute or action for it to constitute valid consideration. That is, there must be some viable argument or challenge to a prior agreement.

What is an illusory promise?

When a promise by one party is subject to a condition that either cannot occur or that is subject to the control of the promising party, the promise is illusory and does not constitute valid consideration.

- *Example*: "If you sing me a song, I will pay you ten dollars if I like your voice." This is a subjective determination (not based on objective criteria) that acts as a condition to the promisor's performance and is thus illusory.

Are exclusive dealing agreements illusory in nature?

No. An exclusive dealing contract generally says that Party 1 will deal exclusively with Party 2, if Party 1 decides to undertake that specific business activity. The fact that one party is limiting itself in its right to deal with other parties constitutes sufficient consideration. Further, courts have interpreted the implied duty of good faith and best efforts in such an agreement as consideration. That is, one party impliedly promises to act in good faith and use best efforts to bring about the situation in which it will deal with the other party.

- *Example*: Party, Inc., enters into an exclusive dealing contract with Singers, LLC, stating that, "Party will exclusively use performing talent from Singers in its party operations." Party is free to not undertake any party operations, but, if it does, it has to work with

Singer. This is an enforceable contract, as Party has forgone a right to use other talent. Singers is obligated under the contract to supply talent to Party in the event Party so demands.

What if a contract states that consideration is rendered, but it is not?

Courts will generally not enforce the contract due to lack of sufficient consideration.

- *Example*: Seller enters into an agreement to sell her home to Buyer. During the due diligence phase, the Buyer notices things about the home that she would like to be fixed. These items are not sufficient to trigger the ability to walk away from the contract. The Seller agrees to make the repairs. The parties enter into a document that says, "for $5 paid, the Seller agrees to make the repairs." The parties never actually exchange the considerations. If the seller fails to make the repairs, she is likely not liable for breach of contract. The court may find the contract unenforceable for lack of consideration.

- *Note*: Options contracts frequently recite consideration that is not given. Courts are split when enforcing or denying enforcement of these agreements. The Restatement generally states that the failure to exchange consideration should not invalidate the contract.

Are any contracts enforceable without consideration?

Statutes and the common law create many scenarios where contracts are enforceable without consideration. The following types of promises are enforceable without consideration:

- Detrimental Reliance: This is an equitable doctrine based upon fairness. It will make an agreement without consideration enforceable where one party justifiably relies on another party's promise and suffers a detriment if the promise is not upheld.

    - *Example*: David tells Grace that he will lend her his tractor. Grace wants to use the tractor to perform some services for a client. Grace relies on David's promise and does not go about renting or purchasing a tractor. On the day of the job, David withdraws his promise to lend Grace the tractor. Grace disappoints the client and is fired from the job. Grace may be able to sue David for breach of contract and the damages she incurred. The promise from David was to make a gift and there was no return promise of performance from Grace. Grace did, however, rely upon David's promise to her detriment. This detrimental reliance may satisfy the requirement for consideration.

- Promise to Pay a Pre-Existing Debt: There is an inference that a party receives something of value by promising to pay a lender a pre-existing debt that is discharged in bankruptcy or barred by a statute of limitations.

    - *Example*: Jane purchases goods on credit from a local antique dealer. She later declares bankruptcy and the debts are discharged through legal proceedings.

Jane later approaches the antique dealer and promises to repay the defaulted debt. This will be a new enforceable agreement.

- <u>Re-affirming a Voidable Promise</u>: If a promisor makes a promise that is voidable because of a lack of mental capacity, mutual mistake, misrepresentation, undue influence, a subsequent promise after the fact may result in an enforceable contract.

  - *Example*: Rayann becomes intoxicated from drinking too much alcohol. During her intoxication, she agrees to give Jan her watch. Once she regains capacity, she quickly repudiates the agreement on the grounds that she lacked capacity to enter into an enforceable agreement. Later, she feels bad about backing out of her promise. She tells Jan that she will indeed give her the watch. This may make the previously voidable agreement enforceable.

- <u>UCC-Specific Transactions</u>: Between merchants, a written release of a claim, a promise not to revoke an offer, and certain contract modifications are enforceable in the absence of considerations.

  - *Example*: Ellie, a merchant, promises to sell Miranda, another merchant, supplies at a given price. Ellie also promises to leave the offer open for 5 days. As previously discussed, this is known as a "firm offer." Even though the promise to leave open the offer is not supported by consideration, it will likely be enforceable under the UCC.

CHAPTER 6: DEFENSES TO ENFORCING A CONTRACT

Understanding the enforceability of a contract requires one to understand certain vocabulary that characterizes the contract.

What is an enforceable and a valid contract?

An enforceable contract is one that courts will order parties to perform or to pay consequences for not performing. A contract is valid when all essential elements are present and it is enforceable. The absence of any key element makes the contract invalid. A contract is unenforceable when the non-performing party has a justifiable reason for non-compliance with the promise.

- *Example*: Naomi agrees to sell Barry a specific piece of equipment for $1,000. The next day, Naomi notifies Barry that she cannot fulfill the contract. Barry is angry and wonders what are his rights in the situation. From the facts, it appears that all of the elements of a valid contract are present. The agreement has an offer, acceptance, and consideration. The contract may not, however, be enforceable. The contract is for the sale of goods for more than $500. As such, the contract must be in writing to be enforceable. If there is not sufficient written evidence of the agreement between the parties to satisfy the statute of frauds, the contract may not be enforceable.

- *Note*: Validity and enforceability are legal terms that have specific definitions. Most legal terms have precise and specific meaning, which is critical when drafting contracts.

What is a void contract?

A void contract is an agreement that lacks an essential requirement for validity and enforceability. An example of a void contract is one that has an illegal purpose or constitutes fraud in the execution. A voidable contract, on the other hand, is an agreement where at least one party has the right to withdraw from the promise made without incurring any legal liability. Defenses that make the contract voidable include, fraud in the inducement, incapacity, duress, mutual mistake, etc.

- *Example*: Michelle enters into an agreement with William to sell him an industrial-grade chemical that is highly regulated and illegal to sell in unauthorized transactions. If the transaction between Michelle and William is not specifically authorized under existing regulations, then it would be illegal. As such, it is a void contract.

A void contract is automatically invalid, whereas a voidable contract is enforceable until a party with the legal right to do so decides to void the contract. Only the innocent party (or party with the defense to enforceability) has the ability to render the voidable contract void. In some cases a contract is voidable by both parties and either one can withdraw. If the innocent party transfers a voidable contract, then the acquiring party loses the right to void the agreement. If the non-innocent party transfers the contract, the innocent party may still void the contract.

The innocent party has the ability to ratify a voidable contract (i.e., make it valid). An innocent party who fails to void the contract upon learning of the defense that makes the contract voidable thereby ratifies the contract.

- *Example*: Tara enters into a contract with Norman while he is intoxicated from taking a prescription medication. As such, the contract is voidable by Norman because, at the time of the agreement, he lacked mental capacity to enter into a contract. Norman must inform Tara of his intent to void the contract very soon upon regaining mental capacity; otherwise, the agreement will be ratified by his failure to give notice of his intention to void it.

What defenses make a contract void (rather than voidable)?

A contract is void if the contract is unconscionable, has an illegal purpose, or its enforcement would violate public policy. Some courts will void the entire contract, while courts in other jurisdiction will sever the void provisions and enforce the other terms. Each of these defenses to contract enforcement is discussed below.

- *Note:* Certain jurisdictions may have laws or regulations that cause an agreement to be illegal or to violate public policy. Further, the standards for what violates public policy is largely based on public sentiment about a particular issue. Naturally, public sentiment changes depending upon the norms, values, culture and customs of a given area.

What is unconscionability?

Unconscionability is when the facts of the contract or the circumstances surrounding its formation make enforcement of the contract "unthinkable." Unconscionability is broken down into procedural and substantive unconscionability.

- *Note*: "Unthinkable" generally means that the contract is so one-sided in nature that it is fundamentally biased in favor of one party against the other party. Further, the reason for the bias is that the agreement is not the product of fair dealing or bargaining between the parties. One party is generally under some form of undue pressure that the favored party uses to her advantage. In essence, the negotiation is tainted and it would violate the purpose of the law to enforce it against the disadvantaged party.

What is procedural unconscionability?

Procedural unconscionability regards the circumstances surrounding the formation of the contract. Basically, one party is presented with a contract in a situation where she lacks a meaningful chance to read, evaluate, or understand those terms. This often comes about when contract terms are written inconspicuously within the contract, such as in the fine print at the bottom of a page. Other unconscionable situations include when the contract is written in dense legalese that is difficult for a person of reasonable intelligence to understand, or presenting the contract to an individual when she lacks the ability to effectively read the contract or is in an extremely imbalanced bargaining position.

- *Example*: Presenting a newby skydiver with a disclaimer once she is in the sky and about to jump out of the airplane for the first time would be unconscionable. The agreement generally biases the skydiver's rights to bring a tort action against the skydiving company. Since the skydiver lacks understanding and a reasonable opportunity to educate herself as to the terms of the agreement, it will likely be unconscionable.

- *Example*: Gina is leaving town to escape a storm coming to the area. The water and power have been shut off from her home. While on the road to evacuate the area, Gina pulls into a hotel to stay for a few hours. The hotel, knowing of Gina's plight, charges her $1,000 per night for the room, rather than the typical $29.99 per night. If Gina enters into a contract to pay the higher rate, she would be able to challenge the enforceability of the agreement due to unconscionability.

What is substantive unconscionability?

Substantive unconscionability is when a contract is so incredibly unfair or oppressive in its terms that it is unthinkable to enforce those terms against a party. This may include a contract that does not provide a party a reasonable remedy under the agreement. Arbitration clauses are routinely challenged on this ground. Some contracts that place extreme penalties or damages for a breach that in no way represents the amount of loss or risk incurred by the parties are deemed substantively unconconscionable. Liquidated damages clauses in contracts are also routinely challenged on this ground. A provision of a contract that produces a huge detriment to one party, without providing the other party a reasonable benefit may also be challenged. Courts may also look at the disparity between the price charged to a customer and the cost of the item to the seller. This may come up in the context of tying arrangements between goods (which is also an antitrust law issue).

- *Example*: Nora signs up for an ocean cruise. She lives in Virginia and the cruise leaves from Florida. The agreement includes an arbitration clause that mandates arbitration of any disputes with arbitrators chosen by the cruise line and located in Oregon. Since nearly all of the passengers live in the Southeastern United States, the choice of Oregon as a forum is used to oppress the customers in any attempt to assert their rights against the cruise line. Nora may be able to challenge the arbitration agreement as being substantively unconscionable.

What is a contract that is illegal or violates public policy?

These contracts either violate a law or promote an objective sought to be reduced or eliminated by law or regulations. Contracts that call for conduct constituting a crime, tort, violation of a regulation or administrative policy, restraint of trade, interference with contractual relations, or violation of consumer protection practices fall in this category. Other contracts that violate public policy are those that include provisions or clauses absolving parties of liability for intentionally harmful conduct.

- *Example*: Sarah is very angry with Cliff. She hires Tommy to beat up Cliff. She agrees to pay Tommy $50 for his services. Before carrying out the assault on Cliff, Tommy has a change of heart and attempts to back out of the deal. Sarah threatens to sue Tommy for his breach of contract. In this situation, the contract between Sarah and Tommy would be void as illegal. You cannot validly contract with someone to commit a crime.

What is mental incapacity and how does it affect contract enforceability?

Mental incapacity of a party to a contract destroys the ability for the parties to have a meeting of the minds. One party lacks the capacity to appreciate the nature and consequences of her actions. Therefore, mental incapacity gives rise to a defense for the incapacitated party and makes it voidable at her choice.

- *Example*: Fran enters into a contract with an encyclopedia salesman when she is temporarily under the influence of prescription medication. Once she regains mental capacity, she will be able to void the contract due to her lack of capacity.

- *Note*: The incapacitated party must void the contract within a reasonable time of regaining capacity and learning of the agreement.

How does mental incapacity affect a minor child's ability to contract?

Most states consider a person below the age of 18 years to be a minor. State statutes deem the minor child to lack the mental capacity to appreciate the nature and consequences of her actions. As such, a contract with a minor child is voidable. This is true even if the minor misrepresents her age at the time of entering the contract. The minor child has the right to void the contract at any time prior to reaching the age of majority and, in most states, for a reasonable time after obtaining majority. Certain contracts for necessities (e.g., food, clothing, shelter) with minors are enforceable to the extent of their fair value.

- *Example:* Clara is 16 and enters into a contract to purchase a new corvette. 10 days after driving off of the car sales lot, she decides to return the car. The dealer does not want to accept return of the car. The dealer sues Clara for breach of contract. Clara will likely be able to defend the action based on the ground that she was a minor and had the right to void the contract at any time before she reaches the age of majority (18 in most states).

- *Note*: If a party is unduly harmed by unknowingly entering into a contract with a minor, the party may have a right of restitution against the minor or her guardian.

How does mental impairment (such as illness) affect a contract?

Mental impairment causes a party to lose the capacity to contract. Contracts entered into during a state of mental impairment are voidable at the insistence of the impaired party. To be eligible to disaffirm the contract, the mentally impaired party must either:

- be in such a state that she cannot understand the nature and consequences of the transaction, OR

- *Example*: Over the years, Ralph has been a collector of antique goods. Ralph now suffers from Alzheimer's disease and can no longer collect these antiques. One day, Donald, a local pawnbroker, visits Ralph and offers to purchase most of his antiques. Ralph agrees to sell him all of the antiques for a given price. Donald is unaware of Ralph's condition at the time of making the offer. In this situation, Ralph (or his appointed guardian) would be able to disaffirm this contract. Ralph lacked the capacity to understand the agreement and can therefore void the contract.

- not be able to perform the contract (and the other party is aware of this inability).

    - *Example*: Derek for years worked as a arborist, specializing in removing large trees in residential neighborhoods. Derek now suffers from Alzheimer's disease, which generally prevents him from practicing his trade. When a local contractor begins building a home in the neighborhood, Ralph approaches the contractor and offers his services to remove a tree that is inconveniently located on the property. The contractor is aware of Ralph's mental illness, but, given the great price, is willing to see if Ralph can do it. The contractor agrees to pay Ralph $1,000 to remove the tree. In this situation, the parties have seemingly entered into a valid contract. Due to Ralph's condition, the contractor knew (or should have known) that Ralph's impairment would prevent him from performing the agreement. As such, Ralph (or his appointed guardian) could disaffirm the contract.

If a party regains his mental capacity before voiding the contract, she must disaffirm the contract within a reasonable amount of time of learning about it. If she fails to do so, she will be deemed to have accepted the contract.

- Note: Examples of situations in which a party is mentally impaired include: dementia, insanity, mental retardation, and intoxication from drugs or alcohol.

What is duress and how does it affect contract enforceability?

Duress is a form of coercion or pressure on another person to take a certain action (such as entering into a contract). Normally, it entails some sort of threat; even though not every threat is improper. If a party claims duress in entering into the contract, the court will look to the facts of the threat to determine whether duress exists. What is the threatening party's purpose in making the threat? If the threat would harm the other party, but would not benefit the threatening party, then it points to duress. The court may examine whether there is a prior history of unfair dealing by the party making the threat that makes it more likely to cause the threatened party to enter into the contract. The court will also determine whether the threat was sufficient to cause the party to unwillingly consent to the contract. The court must make a subjective determination, which means that it is evaluating the situation based upon the age, experience, sophistication, or other general characteristics of the threatened party.

- *Example*: MaryAnn tells Ginger that if she does not sell MaryAnn her hula dress that she will tell the world about Ginger's affair with the Skipper. If Ginger sells MaryAnn her watch, she may be able to later sue to regain the property on the grounds that she entered into the agreement because of duress.

- *Note*: Actions that have been found to constitute duress include: threat of criminal or tortious conduct, extortion of money, threats of a lawsuit that is obviously an abuse of the civil process, blackmail, refusal to perform other valid contracts, and threat of termination of employment. Generally, physical duress is deemed void, while economic duress is generally voidable by the party subject to duress.

What is undue influence and how does it affect contract enforceability?

Undue influence is where one party stands in some position of power or authority over another party and uses that position to coerce the other person's actions. This is very common in fiduciary relationships, such as parent-child, employer-employee, doctor-patient, etc. A party claiming undue influence generally must demonstrate that she was in a position of weakness. The court will determine if any special characteristics of the influenced party (e.g., age, illness, mental state, intoxication, etc.) augmented the possibility that the party was unduly influenced.

- *Example*: The attorney-client relationship is a fiduciary relationship. Contracts between an attorney and client are frequently rendered unenforceable on grounds of undue influence. The burden is on the attorney to demonstrate that the contract was fair, the client was aware of the risks and the attorney's interest in the contract, and the attorney encouraged the client to seek counsel.

When does a mistake by the parties affect contract enforceability?

There are situations where a mistake by one or both parties as to the material facts surrounding the contract can make the contract voidable by one or both parties. Mistakes, in the context of contract enforceability, are generally separated into mutual and unilateral mistake.

What is a mutual mistake and how does it affect contract enforceability?

A mutual mistake is a mistake by both parties about the basic facts or assumptions of the contract. There is variation in the common law as to whether there has to be a mistake in the basic assumptions surrounding the contract or whether the mistake has to concern the subject matter of the contract. In either case, if this misunderstanding materially affects the agreement, the contract is voidable by the adversely affected party.

- *Example*: Tim enters into a contract with Bob to sell him a classic painting that Tim inherited from his grandparents. Tim and Bob both believe that the painting is an early print by famed artist, Auguste Renoir. The parties later find out that the painting is not by Renoir, but is by another famous artist, Claude Monet. The value of the painting is roughly the same. In this case, either party may void the contract, as each party materially misunderstood the terms of the agreement.

When will a unilateral mistake make a contract voidable?

A unilateral mistake about the basic assumptions of the contract will only make the contract voidable when the non-mistaken party knew or had reason to know of the other party's mistake. In such a case, the effect of enforcing the contract against the mistaken party must be unconscionable and the non-mistaken party would not suffer a substantial hardship by voiding the contract. If the non-mistaken party did not know about the other party's mistake, then the standard for voiding the contract is higher. Generally, the contract must not yet have been performed or the parties must be easily restored to their pre-performance positions. The mistake must be substantial, and the mistake must directly relate to some computational or clerical error in the construction of the terms of the agreement.

- *Example*: David enters into an agreement with Alicia to sell her a gold necklace. While David never told her so, Alicia believes that the necklace is made of 24K gold. In reality, the necklace is made of 10K gold and is far less valuable than Alicia believes. When Alicia finds out the true composition of the necklace, she refuses to go through with the contract. If David sues her for breach of contract, Alicia may be able to defend the claim on the grounds that there was a unilateral mistake. Of course, she will likely have to show that David knew about her erroneous belief and that it would cause her a substantial undue hardship.

Are there special situations where a mistake does not give rise to a defense?

Yes. No defense exists if the mistaken party knowingly assumed the risk of the mistake; is grossly negligent in making the mistake; violates a legal duty; fails to act within her duty of good faith and fair dealing; or intentionally fails to read the contract.

- *Example*: Delila enters into a contract to have Jim paint her house. Jim sends her a contract that says that he will use latex paint. After Jim is done painting, Delila says that she assumed that Jim would oil-based paint. She does not want to pay Jim the full price for his services, as she now wants to have the house repainted in oil-based paint. In this case, if Delila intentionally failed to read the contract, she will likely be unsuccessful in asserting a defense of unilateral mistake.

What is misrepresentation and how does it affect contract enforceability?

Misrepresentation is an intentional or unintentional misstatement of facts by a party. If a party enters into a contract based upon a material or fraudulent misrepresentation by another party, then the contract may be voidable by the relying party. The question of voidability turns on whether the misrepresentation was material or whether it was fraudulent. A misrepresentation is material if it would induce a reasonable person into entering the contract, or the misrepresenting party knew or should have know that it would induce the other party. A fraudulent representation is where the misrepresenting party knows that the representation is false and intends to induce the other party into relying on it. Reliance is reasonable if it is based on all of the facts of the situation and subjective characteristics of the deceived party (age, education, experience, etc.).

- *Example*: In an earlier example, Tim enters into a contract with Bob to sell him a classic painting that Tim inherited from his grandparents. In the scenario, Bob and Tim are mistaken about the true artist of the work. If Tim intentionally or inadvertently misrepresents the artist, then Bob would be able to back out of the contract.

- *Note*: Intentional misrepresentation can lead to criminal charges for fraud.

Do opinions or misrepresentations about the state of the law make a contract voidable?

No. Except in limited circumstances, a lack of knowledge of the law (including a misrepresentation by one party to another) is not a defense to a violation of that law. Ignorance of the law is no excuse. Despite this general rule, misrepresentations about the law may make a contract voidable if:

- the misrepresentation is pursuant to a fiduciary relationship or other relationships of trust,

    - *Example*: Jim is an attorney representing Dora in the sale of a business. Jim erroneously informs Dora that the law requires that she undertake numerous legal actions in order to facilitate the sale of the business. As it turns out, the law does not require many of these legal actions. Based upon Jim's advice on the legal process, Dora enters into an agreement to pay Jim $15,000 to assist with the transaction. Dora soon learns that many of the previously discussed legal actions are not necessary. She now believes that she does not really need Jim's assistance with the deal. She attempts to void the contract based on Jim's misrepresentations as to the state of the law. In this case, she will probably be able to do so. As Dora's attorney, Jim is a fiduciary and is thus required to provide an accurate account of the state of the law. In this situation, Dora's mistake as to the state of the law justifies voiding the contract.

- the other party claims to be an expert,

    - *Example*: Todd is a manufacturer of cement building materials. Ellen owns her own environmental consulting business. Ellen approaches Todd and informs him that he is subject to liability under the Environmental Protection Act for failure to conduct routine environmental inspections of his facility. In reality, Todd's type of business is exempt from conducting annual inspections. Todd enters into a contract with Ellen to perform an environmental inspection. Once Tom learns of that the law does not require these inspections, he seeks to void the contract with Ellen based upon mistake of law. Because Ellen held herself out to be an expert in the field, Todd relied upon her in entering the contract. As such, he will likely be able to void the contract.

- the maker has access superior access to the facts of the situation, or

- *Example*: Roger is interested in purchasing Serena's floor cleaning business. Serena discloses all of the information about her cleaning business. As part of this disclosure she states that the cleaning process that the business uses is not subject to regulation by state or federal environmental agencies. Roger enters into a contract with Serena to purchase her business. After entering the contract, Roger learns that the EPA regulates the amount of floor chemical that Serena uses in her scrubbing machines. Serena has consistently exceeded these amounts over the years, and she claims that she was completely unaware of the regulations. Roger is scared that the business will be subject to litigation in future years because of these past practices. Serena's incorrect representation about the state of the law likely makes the contract voidable by Roger.

- *Note*: In the above example, this type of misrepresentation could constitute fraud if Serena knew about the environmental regulation of the product and failed to disclose this information.

- the statement is made by a person posing as a disinterested party.

  - *Example*: Adam visits Pamela's auto sales business. He is interested in purchasing a 1991 model corvette as a hobby car. When talking with Pamela, they begin discussing the insurability of the vehicle and its status as a classic vehicle. One of Pamela's employees poses as a disinterested customer and tells Adam that the corvette definitely qualifies as a classic vehicle for insurance purposes. Later, Adam learns that the corvette is not insurable as a classic car and the insurance rates are incredibly expensive. Because the individual causing the mistake of law was not really a disinterested party (he is an agent of Pamela), this situation may give rise to a claim to void the contract.

Generally, the above exceptions to the general rule that mistakes of law do not make a contract voidable exist to prevent individuals from taking advantage of others who are in special relationships with them.

How does duress or undue influence by a third party affect contract enforceability?

Duress or undue influence by third parties may give rise to a voidable contract. The idea is that there is no mutual assent in a contract entered into as a result of duress or undue influence. As such, the party unduly influenced may void the contract.

- *Example*: John is looking for a supplier of silicone for his toy manufacturing business. One of his current providers of rubber material, RubberTek, offers to supply the silicone at a far higher price than some of the competitors. In negotiating with RubberTek, its agent indicates that RubberTek will stop supplying John with any rubber products if he chooses to purchase silicone from a competitor. This would breach an existing contract that John has with RubberTek; however, RubberTek knows that the interruption may put John out of business. Pursuant to RubberTek's threats, John enters into a contract to purchase the higher-cost silicone. John immediately searches for a new supplier of all rubber material. Once he has done so, he seeks to void the contract with RubberTek. John may be able to void the contract based upon RubberTek's duress in influencing John to enter into the agreement.

- *Note*: The party subject to duress or undue influence must act to void the contract within a reasonable time of the duress or undue influence ending.

What remedies are available to parties to a void contract?

In some cases, the court will review the facts of the situation and make equitable determinations as to the status of the void contract. The court may reform the contract based upon the basic elements of the agreement. Further, the court may make restitution to any parties suffering a detriment under the agreement.

- *Example*: Adrian enters into a contract with Ilene that is rendered void. Under the contract, Adrian performed $500 worth of services for Ilene. Even though the contract is not enforceable, Adrian will likely be entitled to receive from Ilene the reasonable value of her services. This remedy is to avoid Adrian suffering a detriment and Ilene receiving an unfair advantage.

CHAPTER 7: CONTRACTS REQUIRED TO BE IN WRITING – THE STATUTE OF FRAUDS

Do all contracts have to be in writing to be enforceable?

No. Only certain contracts must be in writing to be enforceable. These contracts are required to be in writing pursuant to a doctrine known as the "statute of frauds."

- *Note*: As the name implies, the purpose behind requiring that certain types of contracts be in writing is to prevent fraud by or against parties to the contract. A writing provides the best evidence as to the terms and intentions of the parties to the agreement.

What does the statute of frauds require?

The statute of frauds requires that, in order to be enforceable, certain contracts must meet the following characteristics:

- Be memorialized in a writing or written record (or combination of writings),

    - *Note:* The writing does not have to take the form of a formal contract; rather, it can be any type of physical writing that memorializes the relationship. Handwritten notes, emails, and even text messages could constitute a sufficient writing. The key is that the writings must contain all of the elements described below.

- Identify the parties to the contract,

    - *Note*: Identifying the parties to the contract is a reasonableness standard. It does not necessarily require that the parties use their whole or even real names. It may be the case that the use of nicknames or aliases is sufficient to identify the parties to the agreement.

- Be signed by the party against whom it is being enforced (or her representative), and

    - *Note:* The signature requirement simply means some form of mark or other designation made by the party against whom the contract is being enforced. Handwriting a part of the agreement or initialing any part of the agreement may be sufficient to constitute a signature. Further, using an email address that is password protected may be sufficient to constitute a signature.

- State the essential terms to be performed (specify the quantity of goods to be exchanged).

    - *Note:* Generally, this means identifying the consideration that will be exchanged between the parties.

The absence of any of these elements may cause a court adjudicating a dispute between parties to determine that no valid contract exists or to use default contract provisions to determine the relationship between the parties.

What kinds of contract must be in writing under the statute of frauds?

Several categories of contract uniformly fall under the statute of frauds, including:

- Contracts that, by their terms, cannot be performed within one year of the contract,

    - *Example*: Rick enters into a contract with Lex to provide lawn maintenance for one year. Because it is impossible to complete this contract in less than one year, it is subject to the statute of frauds. This principle generally applies to leases or similar contracts with a stated time period of one year or more.

- Promises to pay or answer for someone else's debts,

    - *Example*: Margaret wants to purchase a vehicle. She has a part-time job and can make the payments, but she does not have much of a credit history. Margaret's mother agrees to guarantee payment of the loan in the event Margaret fails to make payment. This guarantee agreement is a promise to answer for the debts of someone else. As such, it must comply with the statute of frauds to be enforceable.

    - *Note*: Most lenders require that entrepreneurs sign a personal guarantee agreement when their businesses borrow money.

- Promises in consideration of marriage,

    - *Note*: This is a strange example that is a relic of history. It is made to cover situations where a third party promises to transfer something of value to a couple following marriage. Historically, think in terms of a father paying a dowry to the new husband of his daughter.

- The sale of an interest in land (including leases of real property for more than a year),

    - *Example*: Amber wishes to purchase Jaylene's property to build a house. Amber drafts a purchase agreement that identifies the property, the purchase amount, and is then signed by Amber and Jaylene. This written instrument would satisfy the statute of frauds.

    - *Note*: This includes any interest in landing, including the sale of the property, the granting of an easement in the property, selling mineral rights to the property, etc.

- Mortgages,

    - *Note*: Mortgages are loans that are secured by an ownership interest in real estate.

- Contracts for the sale of goods of $500 or more,

    - *Note*: As previously introduced, this is a requirement under section 2-201 of the UCC.

- Lease of goods for $1,000 or more, and

    - *Note*: This provision is located in section 2A-201 of the UCC.

- Security interests in personal property not in the secured party's possession.

    - *Note*: Security interests allow a party a claim to certain property in the event a debt is not paid. Lenders will generally require that a borrower grant the lender a security interest in any property owned by the borrower or to be purchased by the borrower with the borrowed funds.

- *Note*: As previously discussed, contract law is the subject of state law. States have the ability to require that any type of contract be in writing to be enforceable. For example, insurance contracts fall under state law and are required to be in writing. You should review your state's statute of frauds for details when executing any contract.

What type of signature is required for contracts under the statute of frauds?

A writing must either be signed by the party to the contract or her representative. A signature can be any mark or symbol (such as initials or logos) used to identify a party. It may be written, printed, stamped, engraved, or, in some states, electronic. Check individual state rules to determine what types of contracts must be in writing. If the contract consists of multiple writings, only one document needs to be signed if the documents are obviously part of the same transaction.

- *Example*: Whitney enters into a contract to sell her land to Kurt. Her state recognizes an electronic signature as a valid signature. Whitney agrees to sell the land in an email. Later, she decides not to sell the land to Kurt. Kurt sues for breach of contract. Whitney likely will not be able to defend the action based upon the absence of an enforceable contract. Simply sending an email from your personal email address may be sufficient identification to constitute a signature. Further, the court may review multiple emails to piece together the terms of the agreement.

Are there any special signature requirements for merchants?

Yes. Under the UCC, merchants may create an enforceable contract by sending a signed document after the fact to memorialize the contract. The signed writing must be sent within a reasonable time; the receiving party must receive the writing and know it relates to the prior contract, and the receiving party must fail to object to the writing within 10 days of receipt.

- *Example*: Blue, Inc., sends a shipment of material supplies to White, LLC in excess of $500. Both parties are merchants of this type of goods. White did not order these exact supplies. Blue made a mistake in sending these items. After receipt, White realizes that the company can use the supplies. White sends a letter to Blue acknowledging receipt and the intention to retain the supplies. At this point, there is a valid contract arising through the combination of the actions of the parties and a written acknowledgement after the fact.

Can a contract be enforceable if it fails to satisfy the statute of frauds requirements?

Yes. There are numerous exceptions that allow for enforcement of contracts that do not satisfy the statute of frauds requirements. Each type of contract that falls under the statute of frauds has specific exceptions. Some of these exceptions are dealt with individually below.

What statute of frauds exceptions apply to contracts for the sale of goods of $500 or more?

There are several circumstances that allow for partial or full enforceability of these contracts.

- Complete Performance: This is when one or both parties have fully performed the contract (i.e., made payment that is accepted or has delivered goods that were accepted). There may be an enforceable contract for the goods that are delivered or payment made.

    - *Example*: Jovani orders parts from Gloria over the phone for $1,000. Without producing any documents, Jovani ships the parts to Gloria, who accepts them and pays $500. Gloria later decides to return the parts. Jovani has a no-return policy and refuses to accept return of the parts. She sues Jovani for breach of contract, stating that there was no enforceable contract. A court may review the situation and hold the agreement to be enforceable, despite the absence of a written agreement. The actions of Gloria in accepting the subject goods provide sufficient information to reduce the likelihood of fraud in the situation.

- Specialty Goods: If a party enters into a contract for the manufacture and purchase of specialty goods, the contract is enforceable for any of the specialty goods already made by the party. Naturally, there must be some evidence that the specialty goods were intended for the other party.

    - *Example*: Marshal, a musical performer, walks into a jewelry store and asks the owner, Tiffany, to create a custom necklace for him for $100,000. The necklace is made of platinum, has his initials in the center, and is surrounded by precious gems. He makes a down payment, but refuses to sign a contract. Tiffany takes the down payment and begins constructing the necklace. When the necklace is complete, Marshal returns to inspect it. Though the necklace is constructed exactly as Marshal ordered, he does not like the final look and refuses to pay for the item. Tiffany sues Marshal for breach of contract. Marshal attempts to defend against the suit on the grounds that there is no enforceable contract under the statute of frauds. The court may enforce the agreement, despite the absence of a written agreement, because of the special nature of the goods. There is sufficient information in the situation to avoid or reduce the risk of fraud in the transaction.

- <u>Statement Under Oath</u>: If a party admits while under oath in any court proceeding (deposition, pleading, etc.) that the contract existed, then the contract is enforceable to the extent of the admission.

  - *Example*: Zora sues Tom for failure to fulfill his contract obligations. During a deposition, Tom admits that he met with Zora and agreed to sell her the subject products. At trial, he argues that that contract is not enforceable because it lacks a writing sufficient under the statute of frauds. The court can use his statements under oath to enforce the disputed agreement, despite the absence of a written agreement.

What exceptions to the statute of frauds apply to contracts for the sale of real estate?

In contracts for the sale of land, a special exemption exists from the statute of frauds. If a purchaser takes possession of the land and makes permanent improvements, this can be sufficient evidence to take the contract out of the statute of frauds and allow enforcement.

- *Example*: Elaine verbally agrees to sell Elijah a piece of real estate. Pursuant to this verbal agreement, Elijah makes a down payment and takes possession of the land. Elijah has the land surveyed and graded to build a house. Later, Elaine decides to back out of the deal on the grounds that there is not a contract enforceable under the statute of frauds. In this situation, a court may hold that an enforceable contract exists based upon this exception to the statute of frauds.

- *Note*: This situation can also give rise to a detrimental reliance claim to establish an implied-in-law contract or a claim for restitution for the value of work put into improving the property.

What exceptions to the statute of frauds apply to contracts with durations of more than 12 months?

In contracts with a duration of more than one year, substantial performance of the contract may be sufficient to allow for continued enforceability. Further, once the contract is fully performed, the statute of frauds does not prevent posthumous enforcement of any details.

- *Example*: Frank enters into a lawn service agreement with Elizabeth that will last for two years. After 10 months, Elizabeth seeks to get out of the agreement. When she fails to pay her monthly bill, Frank sues her. Elizabeth defends the action by arguing that there is not an enforceable contract under the statute of frauds. The court may side with Frank, as the agreement has been substantially performed for a significant period of time. The extent of services provided to Elizabeth over this period of time and the history of payments is likely sufficient to demonstrate that a contract indeed existed. This information greatly reduces the likelihood of fraud in the agreement. Of course, there will still need to be evidence indicating that the contract was for 2 years.

What is promissory estoppel?

This is yet another exception to the statute of frauds. All contracts are subject to equitable (fairness) principles. Most notably, the principle of promissory estoppel can make contracts enforceable that do not meet statute of frauds requirements. The promissory estoppel doctrine means that, based upon principles of fairness and equity, one party may be estopped (or stopped) from denying that a contract indeed exists. Under this equitable principle, the statute of frauds does not bar enforcement of a contract if:

1) The promisor states that a writing will be made and fails to produce the writing,

    - *Example*: Winston agrees to sell horse feed at a given price to Rashad. Winston states that he will work up a contract for the sale. Despite Rashad's insistence, Winston fails to produce the contract.

OR

2) The promisor induces action (or inaction) by the party seeking enforcement,

    - *Example*: Calvin tells John that he will sell John the supplies necessary to complete a work contract. He tells John to go ahead and plan on having the supplies necessary to complete the entire contract. John relies on Calvin's representation by not securing the supplies from another supplier.

AND

3) The party seeking enforcement relies on this representation to her detriment.

    - *Example*: In either of the above situations, there could be a legal detriment suffered by the party seeking an exception to the statute of frauds if Winston or Calvin fail to perform. If Rashad is unable to secure feed or Calvin is unable to secure materials, they may suffer a detriment. Further, they could suffer a detriment if the cost of feed or supplies has risen since the time of entering into the original agreements.

    - *Note*: The detriment suffered by one party must be a direct result of the other party's failure to perform her obligations under the agreement. The detriment does not, however, have to be the subject of the agreement. As in the above example, the detriment can be the result of an inability to perform a second and independent agreement.

Generally, the court will use this exception when fairness dictates that enforcing the contract is the only reasonable means of avoiding injustice to the relying party.

- *Note*: Some courts have refused to apply promissory estoppel principles to contracts under the UCC, because the UCC includes enumerated exceptions to the statute of frauds.

CHAPTER 8: CONTRACTS & THIRD PARTIES – RIGHTS & DUTIES

Do third parties have any right to enforcement a contract to which they are not parties?

A third party may enforce a contract in which she has rights. She only has rights in a contract if the parties to the contract intend to benefit the third party at the time of entering the contract and that intent is manifest within the agreement. A third party may also acquire rights in an already executed contract if one party to the contract validly transfers those rights to the third party. The extent of the third party's rights is determined by their status as donee beneficiary or creditor beneficiary.

- *Example*: Bill enters into a requirements contract with Elaine to purchase all of the widgets that Elaine produces. Hank enters into a supply contract with Elaine to supply her with all of the materials necessary to make the widgets that Elaine sells to Bill. Elaine is Hank's only customer for these materials. When entering the contract, he is aware of the quantity of product demanded by Bill and how much material Elaine will need to fulfill that contract. He develops his operations to meet that need. Later, Bill breaches his requirements contract with Elaine and begins to purchase widgets from other producers. While Elaine may sue Bill for breach of contract, Hank has no rights to enforce the contract against Bill because he is not an intended beneficiary under that contract.

What contractual rights does a donee beneficiary have?

A donee beneficiary is a third party who receives contractual rights as a gift from the promisee. If a promisee makes a contract for the benefit of a donee beneficiary and the promisor fails to perform, the third-party may not bring an action against the promisee, but may bring an action against the promisor. Since the transfer to the beneficiary is a gift, there are no grounds for recourse against the promisee.

- *Example*: Duval enters into a contract to sell 30 bags of cement to Robert. Robert pays Duval for the cement and transfers the right to receive the 30 bags of cement to Clint as a gift. Duval fails to deliver the cement to Clint. Clint is not an intended beneficiary under the contract; however, Robert validly transfers his rights under the contract to Clint. As such, Clint is a donee beneficiary and now stands in the shoes of Robert with regard to the contract. Clint may sue Duval for breach of contract. Clint may not sue Robert for the failed delivery, as the transfer of the right to receive bags of cement is simply a gift.

What contractual rights does a creditor beneficiary have?

A creditor beneficiary is a third party who receives contractual rights from the promises as satisfaction of a debt. When a promisor fails to perform under the subject contract, the creditor beneficiary can bring an action against the promisee and the promisor. The promisee may also bring an action against the promisor, as her rights have been harmed by the promisor's failure to perform.

- *Example*: In the above example, Clint is a donee beneficiary, as he acquired the right to receive the bags of cement as a gift. Now suppose that Robert transfers his rights to Clint in order to satisfy a gambling debt that he owes to Clint. In that case, Clint will be able to sue Robert for failure to pay the gambling debt (the transfer of rights is without value) or sue Duval for failure to perform the contract. Since the contract was not performed, Robert still owes Clint and has not received the 30 bags of cement that he paid for. As such, Robert may sue Duval for breach of contract.

- *Note*: In the above example, if Clint and Robert both sue Duval, the court will only allow one party to recover. In such a situation, the court would consolidate the legal action into a single proceeding in order to adequately deal with all parties' rights and interests.

When can a third-party beneficiary prevent modification of a contract to which she is a beneficiary?

Third-party beneficiaries may be able to prevent the parties to the contract from modifying (or rescinding) the contract without their consent. The third-party beneficiary's authority in this regard depends upon her status as a donee or creditor beneficiary. Further, it depends upon when the third party's rights have vested.

- *Note*: Each state has its own rules for when contractual rights vest in third parties. Some states apply these rules uniformly to donee and creditor beneficiaries, while other states vary the vesting time depending on that type of beneficiary.

In general, a donee beneficiary's consent is required to modify the contract at the time when her rights vest in the contract. Her rights vest either when the rights are transferred to her and she learns about it or when her rights are expressly reserved in the contract.

- *Example*: Tamra enters into a contract to trade widgets with Douglas. Douglas transfers his right to receive Tamra's widgets to Louise. He notifies Louise of his intended gift *via* standard mail. Tamra and Douglas may modify the contract at any time prior to Louise's receipt of notice of the gift. Once Tamra receives notice of her gift (assuming the gift is already transferred), Tamra and Douglas cannot modify the contract in a manner that would detriment Louise's rights.

The creditor beneficiary's rights in the contract vest either:

- when the contract is made,
    - *Note*: This is the case when the third-party beneficiary is named in the contract,
- when the third party learns of the contract and does not expressly reject the benefits, or
    - Note: This situation is the same as that of a donee beneficiary,
- when the third party takes action in reliance on those benefits.

- *Note*: This is the equitable doctrine of detrimental reliance.

As with the donee beneficiary, once a creditor beneficiary's rights have vested, the original parties cannot modify or rescind a contract in such a manner that would diminish the third party beneficiary's rights without her consent.

Can contracts be assigned to other parties?

Assignment is the transfer by one party of her right to receive performance from the other party to the contract. As discussed above, assignments can be a gift or an exchange for other value. In general, unless the contract deems otherwise, obligors and obligees may assign their rights or duties under the contract to third parties (assignees). The assignor must give notice to the other party immediately upon assignment.

- *Example*: Will owes Eric monthly recurring revenue payments pursuant to a royalty agreement. Eric transfers the right to receive the royalties to Wynona. Eric must notify Will of the assignment in order to obligate Will to make payments to Wynona.

- *Note*: In most states, if a party makes an offer of assignment to multiple assignees, the assignee who first notifies the obligor of the assignment has priority in the contract benefits.

What is required to assign a contract?

A contract can be assigned through agreement between the assignor and assignee. Assignments of common law contracts do not have to be in writing. Assignments of contracts for the sale of goods must be in writing if the original contract was subject to the statute of frauds.

- *Example*: Jimmy enters into a contract to supply Lia with silicon microchips for use in hand-held computing devices that she produces. The value of the products is $50,000. Lia prepays for a certain amount of inventory. Lia later merges her business with Sarah's business. She transfers the rights to receive the silicon microchips to Sarah. The original contract is subject to the statute of frauds, so the assignment to Sarah must also comply with the statute of frauds to be effective.

- *Note*: An assignment between the assignor (a party to the contract) and an assignee (the person receiving the assignment) is an independent or collateral contract to the original contract between the parties.

Are there contracts that cannot be assigned?

Yes, some contracts cannot be assigned. A contract that materially alters the obligor's duties under the agreement is not transferable. For example, an assignment that varies greatly a party's delivery requirements cannot be assigned. Doing so may detriment the obligor who has to meet a new (and possibly more taxing) delivery schedule.

- *Example*: Robert agrees to paint Samantha's house for a given price per square foot of the house. Samantha decides to sell her home and attempts to gift the service to her brother Will. Will's house is far larger than Samantha's home and is far more difficult to paint. Samantha would not be able to transfer this contract; as such a transfer would considerably increase Robert's duties.

Generally, any contract that materially increases the other party's burden, risk, or ability to receive return performance is not assignable. For example, requirement contracts cannot be assigned because the producer's duty depends on the individual output requirements of the purchaser.

- *Example*: Ilsa enters into a contract with Gabbi to supply all of the bricks that her construction business needs. Gabbi attempts to transfer the contract to Harold. Harold's construction business is far larger than that of Gabbi and requires far more bricks. This would create an undue hardship on Ilsa, who has to meet a higher level of performance. As such, the assignment will likely not be enforceable.

Lastly, a party to a contract cannot assign (delegate) performance of duties under a contract when performance depends on the character, skill, or training of that party. For example, one singer cannot transfer her obligations under a contract to another singer if the other party depended upon the skill of that particular vocalist.

- *Example*: Katy Perry enters into a contract to perform at the Super Bowl. One week before the event, Katy attempts to transfer the contract to Justin Bieber. Even though both performers are extremely popular, the contract cannot be assigned. The reason is because the nature of the contracted services depends entirely on the individual skill and reputation of the individual artist. Substituting another artist does not replace that part of the bargain.

- Note: This topic is discussed further below in the context of delegation.

Can a contract be assigned to multiple parties?

A party can partially assign a contract or assign the same contract to multiple parties. Different jurisdictions follow different rules regarding the priority of the assignees. Some jurisdictions allow that the first assignee of a contract who gives notice to the obligor has priority over other assignees.

- *Example*: Tom performed services for Payments, Inc., and now has a right to receive three monthly payments of $2,500. Tom transfers this right to receive payments to Anna. He later assigns the same rights to Brad. Brad is the first person to notify Payments, Inc., of the assignment. As such, Brad has priority in the right to payment. Anna will have no legal recourse against Payments, Inc., for failure to make payments to her.

Other jurisdictions follow the rule that the first assignee to receive assignment of a contract has priority to performance by the obligor.

- *Example*: Pursuant to this rule, Anna would have priority over Brad. If Payments, Inc., makes payment to Brad instead of Anna, she would have a cause of action against it.

Still other jurisdictions follow the rule that the first assignee has priority, unless a later assignee:

- pays value for the assignment in good faith without notice of a prior assignment (and the prior assignee did not receive the assignment in good faith and for value),
  - *Note:* This principle is known as a "purchaser in good faith" or a "good faith purchaser for value."
  - *Example*: In the above scenario, if Brad pays Tom for assigning the payment rights to him without notice that he has assigned the rights to Anna, he will have priority over Anna. This scenario assumes that Anna did not pay value for the assignment; otherwise, Anna would retain priority.
- receives a judgment against the obligor,
  - *Note*: If a court adjudicates the matter, it may be vested with the authority to establish priority of ownership in the payments.
  - *Example*: Anna would have priority, unless Brad begins a legal action in which the court orders that Payments, Inc., pay the funds to Brad.
- executes a novation, or
  - *Note*: A novation is a new contract between individuals that replaces a party to the contract or obligations or rights under the agreement.
  - *Example*: Brad may have priority if he enters into a direct contract with Payments, Inc., that supersedes the old contract with Tom. Generally, Tom must agree to formation of this new contract.
- receives a written assignment capable of transfer.
  - *Note*: Some agreements, such as assignments that are subject to the statute of frauds, are only capable of being assigned *via* a valid writing. If a prior assignment does not satisfy the statute of frauds, a subsequent transfer could take precedent.
  - *Example*: The agreement between Payments, Inc., and Tom was for a stated duration of more than one year. As such, it was subject to the statute of frauds. If the assignment of rights under the contract to Anna was verbal, then it may not

be enforceable. If, however, the second assignment to Brad complies with the statute of frauds, it may have priority over Anna's assignment.

It is important to review the specific rules applicable to the specific jurisdiction when determining one's rights under an assigned contract.

Can an assignment be revoked?

A gratuitous assignment cannot be revoked if the assignment is made pursuant to a written document signed by the assignor. If no writing exists, revoking a gratuitous assignment is extremely easy. It can be revoked by an assignor later assigning the same right (the last assignment controls), the death or incapacity of the assignor, or by the delivery of notification of revocation to the assignee or obligor.

- *Example:* Crystal verbally assigns her rights under a contract to William. Later, Crystal sends a written notification to Thomas that she is assigning those same rights to Thomas. She then notifies the obligor that she has assigned the rights to Thomas. The assignment to Crystal is revoked. The same would be true if she sent notice to William.

- *Note:* Certain circumstances between the obligor and assignee may also make the assignment irrevocable, including the receipt of payment or other satisfaction of the obligation, obtaining a judgment on the contract against the obligor, the obligor and assignee entering into a novation, or detrimental reliance by the assignee.

A contract exchanged for value cannot be revoked.

Can a contract be modified after assignment?

Generally, no. As previously discussed, once a contract has vested, the parties generally cannot modify the contract in a way that impairs the assignee's rights. If, however, a modification does not affect the assignee's rights, then it may be modified. In some cases, the assignee can effectively alter the contract by disclaiming her rights under the agreement.

- *Example*: Richard enters into a contract to provide services to Sammy. Richard assigns his right to receive payments under the contract to Bernice in full payment of an existing debt. Richard and Sammy cannot modify the contract if that modification would affect Bernice's rights. They would, however, be able to modify the contract to alter the location of services, if that change of location does not detriment Bernice.

- *Note*: There is an exception in commercial contracts that allows for modifications or substitutions in accordance with commercially acceptable standards. This allows for slight modifications that are within the expectations of the parties.

Can a party delegate duties under a contract?

Generally, unless the parties agree otherwise, a party can delegate her obligations or duties under a contract. Most jurisdictions require that the delegatee receive any benefits from the delegation and not suffer a detriment in any way. If, however, the contract calls for personal services that rely on the subjective skill or ability of the obligor, then the contract cannot be delegated.

- *Example*: Brad owns a music store. He gives lessons and sells musical equipment. He enters into a contract to sell instruments to the local high school and the agreement does not contain a "no-assignment/delegation clause." He also has contracts with multiple students to provide music lessons. When Brad decides to sell his store, he delegates the sales contract to the purchaser. He cannot, however, transfer the services contract without the consent of the music students. The lessons he provides generally require a unique or subjective skill set. Such service contracts cannot be delegated without the consent of the other party to the agreement.

Is a delegator relieved of responsibility after delegating the contract?

No. The party delegating the contract is still potentially liable under the contract if the delegatee fails to perform. If, however, the delegatee and the obligee under the contract enter into a novation, then the delegator is relieved of responsibility. If the delegator expresses her intent to repudiate the contract upon assignment to the delegatee, then there is an implied novation if the obligee does not object.

- *Example*: Zach enters into a lawn service contract to maintain Phillis' yard. Zach delegates performance to Jason, who has just started his lawn maintenance business. If Jason fails to perform under the agreement, Zach could still potentially be liable to Phillis. To be relieved from potential liability, Phillis and Jason must re-affirm the existing contract or enter into a new contract that supersedes the original agreement with Zach. This is known as a novation. Zach should announce his delegation of the contract and his intention to be relieved from liability on the agreement. If Phillis does not object, then there is an implied novation.

Is the delegatee liable under the contract if no novation takes place?

It depends. The delegatee will be liable under the contract if she expressly or impliedly accepts responsibility for performance. In this case both the delegating party and the delegatee may be liable on the contract.

- *Example*: In the above example, Jason now holds the contract to maintain Phillis' yard. If there is no novation, then Jason is only liable if he expressly or impliedly assumes responsibility for the services. This includes any form of acknowledgement to Phillis that he will be responsible for servicing her yard.

CHAPTER 9: INTERPRETING CONTRACTUAL TERMS

What general principle(s) are used in interpreting contractual provisions?

The majority of jurisdictions interpret contract provisions based upon their "plain meaning." That is, if a contract term is unambiguous, then the court will apply the meaning commonly applied to the term or provision.

- *Example*: Marcus manufactures widgets and enters into a contract to sell some widgets to Melvin. In the contract, Marcus agrees to "scrub" all of the widgets to remove any unwanted dirt or debris from manufacturing. When Melvin receives the widgets, the widgets appear to still have a thin layer of undesirable oil residue from the manufacturing process. Melvin asserts to Marcus that he has definitely not scrubbed the widgets as required by the contract, as evidence by the oil residue. Marcus replies that he subjected the widgets to a cold, spray-washing process, which is the equivalent of scrubbing them and that the oil residue is not his problem. Melvin refuses to pay for the widgets and Marcus sues him for breach of contract. Melvin asserts a defense that Marcus breached the contract by failing to "scrub" the widgets. The court may interpret the word "scrub" by its plain meaning, to determine who first breached the contract.

- *Note*: The court will generally assume that a contract contains all relevant terms and that there are no contemporaneous or prior terms or pieces of the contract that are part of the agreement. A contract that contains all relevant terms and provisions is known as a "complete integration."

Other jurisdictions interpret contract provisions based upon how a "reasonable person" in those circumstances would interpret the contract. This is known as the "objective standard."

- *Example*: In the above situation, the court would place itself in the shoes of a reasonable person to determine what the parties meant by including the word scrub. If a reasonable person would believe that "scrub" includes subjecting to a cold spray-wash, then Melvin may prevail in the lawsuit.

- *Note*: Generally, if the contract has an "integration clause" and it does not contain any ambiguous terms or provisions, then the court will employ the objective or reasonable person standard in interpreting the contract. An integration clause is a contractual provision that states that the contract contains all of the terms of agreement between the parties and no outside evidence not specifically mentioned in the agreement should be considered. If the contract does not have an integration clause and/or it appears ambiguous, then the court will take into consideration the subjective intent of the parties when interpreting the contract. This means that the court will look, not at how a reasonable person would interpret the applicable term or provision, but at how the parties themselves interpreted the provision.

Finally, some jurisdictions will look to any outside evidence to determine the subjective intent of the parties.

- *Example*: In the case of Marcus and Melvin, the court would accept any outside evidence that the parties could offer to demonstrate what meaning the parties attributed or should have attributed to the word "scrub."

- *Note*: In such jurisdictions, whether the contract has an integration clause is irrelevant.

Do courts employ any rules to aid the interpretation of contracts?

Yes. Each state or individual jurisdiction employs any number of general rules in the interpretation of contracts. These rules are generally established through prior judicial precedent (common law) or practice within the jurisdiction. Some common approaches to interpreting contract provisions are as follows:

- Interpret terms to give them a reasonable meaning;

    - *Note*: Reasonable meaning depends upon the plain definition of the word and the context of the contract. Given the situation, the court will determine what meaning is reasonable in light of the circumstances.

- Afford the greatest weight to the contract's express terms;

    - *Note*: The express terms of the contract will have the greatest weight and will guide the interpretation of any meaning that is implied from those terms. Nothing will be implied that contradicts the express terms.

- Look to implied terms originating from the course of dealing, course of performance, or trade usage;

    - *Note*: If the express terms are not conclusive, the court will look toward these factors to determine what is implied by the express terms of the agreement.

- Give greater weight to specific terms above general terms;

    - *Note*: An express contract term will not be contradicted by more general provisions of the agreement.

- Terms that are actually negotiated between the parties are given greater weight than standard terms or boilerplate;

    - *Note*: The action provisions, representations, warranties, and conditions will be preferred above the general provisions of the agreement.

- The court will take into consideration the overall circumstances of the agreement;

- *Note*: The court may look at all of the factors surrounding the agreement. This could include the parties, the industry, the subject-matter of the agreement, the objective to be achieved by the agreement, etc.

- The purpose of the contract, if ascertainable, should be considered in interpreting the intentions of the parties;

    - *Note:* This regards what the parties hope to achieve through the agreement. For example, if the agreement is a supply contract, the parties intend to supply all of the needed product at a given price.

- Interpret all parts of the contract as a whole (including when the contract consists of multiple writings);

    - *Note*: The court will look to interpret all portions of the writing collectively, rather than look at individual provisions in isolation.

- Words are given their prevailing meaning in the context of the contract;

    - *Note*: What is the standard for this type of provision or term in similar types of contracts.

- Specific trade terms are to be interpreted in accordance with their meaning in the trade;

    - *Note*: The court looks specifically to the trade or industry usage of these types of terms or provisions.

- The parties' intentions are interpreted consistently and in accordance with course of performance, dealing, and trade usage; and

    - *Note*: The court will look specifically to the prior dealings between the parties in this and previous deals. It will also look to general agreements of this nature within the trade or industry.

- Ambiguous terms may be interpreted against the drafter.

    - *Note*: The drafter has the last opportunity to avoid ambiguous terms or provisions. The failure to avoid these situations is held against the drafter.

What is the significance of a prior course of performance, dealing, or trade usage in interpreting a contract?

All of the above rules provide context for interpreting the contract. Often, express terms (terms written or expressed in the agreement) are difficult to interpret. These factors may provide clarity. Also, these factors may serve to fill in inferred or implied meaning in the contract that is not expressed. For example, some courts will interpret a contract to impliedly include additional terms that are not specifically stated in the contract.

What is course of performance and dealing?

Courses of performance and dealing mean any actions taken by a party in carrying out the contract or in prior dealings leading up to the present contract. In cases where a contract is on-going (such as a supply contract) or broken into pieces (such as an installment contract), any prior activity in carrying out any portion of the contract (the "course of performance") can provide context, meaning, and additional terms to the contract. Likewise, previous contract agreements or interactions by the parties outside of the contract may provide such context (the "course of dealing").

- *Example*: Cameron has long-standing, business dealings with Jade. Cameron has purchased supplies from Jade for several years. In a recent supply contract, Cameron refuses to accept a shipment of supplies due to the tardiness of arrival. When Jade sues Cameron for a breach of contract, the parties argue over the provision in the contract requiring that shipment of supplies be received by Cameron "within a timely period." Cameron says that the shipment was not made "within a timely period," which she concludes is a breach of contract excusing her from the duty to accept the goods. In interpreting the contract, the court may look at the prior course of dealing between the parties to determine the meaning of "within a timely period." If the Cameron accepted supplies in the past that were equally tardy in arrival, then it may be reasonable to interpret the provision to include the present time period. If so, Cameron may have breach the contract by failing to accept the supplies.

- *Example*: In the above situation, let's assume that the contract is an installment contract. The shipment in question is the third in a series of shipments. If Cameron routinely accepted prior shipments without objections, then this would influence the courts interpretation of the current situation. The course of performance of the contract may indicate that Jade is indeed delivering goods "within a timely period."

- *Note*: If, when entering the contract, a party expressly objects to considering any prior performance or dealing by the parties in interpreting the contract, the court generally will not use course of performance in interpreting the agreement.

What is trade usage and why is it important?

Specific terms, provisions, phrases, etc., have special meaning in a given trade or business. Any such meaning can influence the contract, as the court may accept the definition or meaning of a word or phrase as it is commonly understood in that trade or business.

- *Example*: Tom, an attorney, argues to the court for a ruling based upon equity (fairness). Sharon, a stock trader, sells equity (ownership interest) in businesses. These are the same words, but have different meanings in specific industries. A court would interpret these contracts differently depending on the context of the contract (a legal agreement or a stock-trading agreement).

What is the parole evidence rule?

This rule or doctrine controls whether parties may introduce to the court interpreting the contract evidence of their agreement that is not included within the written document. This rule either allows or disallows a party from introducing that evidence to the court to modify or add terms to a contract.

- *Example*: Kate sues Sally for breach of contract. Sally defends this assertion by by claiming that the provision was not meant to be in the agreement. Sally wants the court to consider several communications between herself and Kate prior to the contract in an attempt to show that she did not breach the provision. If the prior communications contradict the terms that are expressly present in the contract, the court may not accept the evidence based upon the parole evidence rule.

- *Note*: Parties generally negotiate a contract prior to finalizing the terms in a written agreement. The parole evidence rule primarily serves to exclude any evidence of prior negotiations (either before or contemporaneous with the signing of the contract) that have the effect of altering the express terms of the agreement. The purpose of this rule is to prevent confusion in the interpretation of the contract and fraud by any party against another. Information or communications contemporaneous with execution of the contract may be admissible in interpreting the contract, but are not admissible if they expressly contradict unambiguous, contract terms.

When does the parole evidence rule apply to a contract?

The contract must be the final agreement between the parties. If the party is determined to be a final expression of the parties' agreement, then the parole evidence rule is effective to limit what information outside of the writing the parties can introduce to the court in interpreting the agreement.

- *Example*: In the above example of Kate and Sally, the court will determine whether the contract is a complete and final expression of the parties' agreement. Often a contract will have a clause stating that the document is a complete and final expression of the agreement between the parties. This is known as an "integration clause" and is discussed below. A complete and final agreement may also be evident by the terms and structure of the agreement.

- *Note*: As indicated in the above example, the courts may interpret a contract to be the complete and final agreement between the parties. The best way to make certain that the contract is deemed a complete and final expression of the parties' intent is to include an "integration clause."

What is "integration" and why is this concept important to contract interpretation?

As stated above, a contract must be final for the parole evidence rule to apply. Integration means that all of the facts or information constituting the agreement between the parties are present in the written agreement.

- *Example*: Grace enters into a contract with Will to provide him with design services. The contract does not make reference to any outside agreements. It appears by all accounts to address all of the terms of the agreement within the written document. As such, the contract would likely be deemed an integration for interpretation purposes.

- *Note*: An agreement may appear on its face as simply a partial understanding of the agreement between the parties. In such as case, the contract is not an integration. If a court determines that the document is an integration, it can either be completely integrated or partially integrated.

What is a complete integration and why does it matter?

A complete integration is when the contract contains all of the facts or information regarding the parties' agreement. If the court determines that a contract is a complete integration, the parole evidence rule limits all prior or contemporaneous outside evidence that contradicts, modifies, or supplements the contract.

- *Example*: In the previous example of Kate and Sally, the court will not allow Sally to introduce the prior communications that in any way contradict, modify, or supplement the contract. There is a limited use for such communications to clarify ambiguous terms, as discussed below.

- *Note*: A complete integration will generally contain a strong integration clause specifically excluding any outside information not specifically mentioned in the terms of the agreement.

What is partial integration and why does it matter?

The written document may contain only part of the information constituting the agreement between the parties. If a court determines that a contract is a partial integration, it will allow certain outside evidence that serves to supplement or explain provisions of the contract. Even with a partial integration, the parole evidence rule restricts outside evidence of prior or contemporaneous communications that specifically contradict the terms of the contract.

- *Example*: In the situation of Kate and Sally, the court will allow the prior communications if they somehow supplement the terms of the contract or explain terms therein. These communications will not be admissible, however, if they contradict express terms or provisions of the contract.

- *Note*: Partial integrations generally do not contain integration clauses. Often, the agreement itself will make reference to outside communications to clarify certain provisions of the agreement.

How does the court determine if a writing is a partial or complete integration?

Courts employ a number of approaches in determining whether an integration exists and, if so, whether it is a partial or complete integration. The dominant approaches are as follows:

- Reasonable Person Approach – The court looks at the contract to determine if a reasonable person would believe the agreement to be a complete expression of all of the terms between the parties (complete integration). If there is evidence of outside terms, the court will look to determine whether the outside terms were meant to be a part of the agreement or whether they would typically form a separate agreement. If they were not intended to be a part of the agreement, then there may be an integration. If they are terms that are typical or common to have in a separate agreement, then the court may find that the document is partially integrated. As previously discussed, a partial integration allows the introduction of prior or contemporaneous terms that do not contradict the existing terms of the contract.

    - *Note*: The reasonable person approach is the most common approach across jurisdictions.

- Plain meaning Approach – The court will look at the terms of the contract and interpret them in accordance with their plain meaning. The plain meaning may include taking into consideration the context of the contract. If the document appears to be a complete and final expression of the agreement between the parties, then it is presumed to be a complete integration.

    - *Note*: While there is a presumption of complete integration, the party seeking to introduce external evidence into the agreement may rebut this presumption through any means available.

- Collateral Contract Approach – This approach to determining integration assumes that all final writings are partial integrations. As such, the court will entertain the introduction of outside evidence that does not contradict or add to the express terms of the agreement. Such information is simply seen as a collateral contract or agreement that may affect the interpretation of the present agreement.

    - *Note*: The introduction of these outside terms may demonstrate that an ambiguity exists in the contract. In such as case, the court may employ the information to resolve any conflicts surrounding the ambiguity.

- Intention of the Parties Approach – The court, under this approach, will allow the introduction of any evidence deemed relevant to the determination of the existence of a contract. This approach offers the greatest latitude in the introduction of prior negotiations or communications between the parties.

- Note: Aspects of this approach are present in both the Restatement and UCC.

What is an integration clause and how does it relate to integration?

An integration clause, also called a "merger clause," is a provision in a contract that says that the contract is a complete and final understanding of all the terms of the agreement. In other words, these clauses state that the contract is intended to be a complete integration. Some merger clauses will specifically state that any outside information or communications contemporaneous with the execution of the contract or prior thereto should not be considered a part of the contract. Other, more specific clauses, will specifically reference outside information, documents, or communications and state whether the terms of those items are included in the final agreement.

- *Example*: "This Contract contains the entire agreement of the parties with respect to the subject matter of the Contract. The contract supersedes any prior agreements, understandings, or negotiations, whether written or oral. This Contract can only be amended through a written document formally executed by all parties."

- *Note*: These clauses are usually conclusive unless a contract defense applies (such as fraud, duress, etc.).

When does the parole evidence rule not bar the consideration of extrinsic evidence to a contract?

As previously stated, the parole evidence rule applies to a complete integration to limit the court's consideration of any prior or contemporaneous information in interpreting a contract. The parole evidence rule, however, does not bar extrinsic evidence offered for the following purposes:

- to aid in the interpretation of existing terms (for example, when an ambiguity exists),

- to show that a writing is or is not an integration,

- to establish that an integration is complete or partial,

- to establish subsequent agreements or modifications between the parties (i.e., those arising after the contract is completed), or

- to show that the terms of the contract were the product of illegality, fraud, duress, mistake, lack of consideration or other invalidating cause.

- *Note*: These exceptions exist to reduce misunderstanding and fraud between the parties and to promote judicial efficiency in the interpretation of agreements.

How can extrinsic evidence be used to clear up ambiguities?

As stated above, extrinsic evidence or information prior to or contemporaneous with the formation of the contract cannot be introduced to contradict the contract. One exception to this rule is the use of extrinsic evidence to determine the meaning the parties attribute to certain terms or provisions. Generally, a court will give a term its common meaning or the meaning common in the context of the contract (such as a particular trade usage). Nonetheless, often a term or provision of the contract will be ambiguous. In such a case, it may be necessary to employ extrinsic evidence or information from outside of the contract to determine the intentions or meaning attributed by the parties.

- *Example*: Clarence enters into a contract with Audrey to sell and deliver specially-manufactured widgets. The contract states that Clarence will "deliver the widgets to Audrey's place of business." Audrey has multiple places of business, including a central administrative office, but the contract does not differentiate these locations. Audrey is not happy when Clarence delivers the widgets to the headquarters, rather than to one of her retail business locations. Audrey sues Clarence for breach of contract. The court may determine that the phrase "place of business" is ambiguous. It could mean any of Audrey's business locations, or it could mean one of the retail locations. In such a situation, the court may allow extrinsic evidence to show an ambiguity exists or to explain the parties' original understanding. Clarence may be able to produce a prior communication where he specifically states that he will deliver the goods to the headquarters location.

- *Note*: Ambiguities are broken into latent and patent ambiguities.

What is a patent and latent ambiguity?

Generally, outside evidence may be introduced to clear up an ambiguity that is obvious on the face of the document. This is known as a "patent" ambiguity. If a party claims that the contract contains an ambiguous term, but it is not obvious on the face of the contract, then the party is claiming that a latent ambiguity exists. In such a case the party may be able to introduce outside evidence to show that an ambiguity exists. If the court determines that an ambiguity exists, it may consider extrinsic evidence to resolve the ambiguity.

- *Example*: In the above example of Clarence and Audrey, Audrey may introduce evidence to show that the parties specifically referred to her headquarters location as "headquarters." The parties specifically differentiate this location from her retail locations, which are referred to as her "businesses." In such a situation, this information would demonstrate that the meaning ascribed to "place of business" in the contract is ambiguous. As such, this may justify the introduction of additional external evidence to determine the meaning attributed to the term by the parties.

- *Note*: Many courts may not distinguish between patent and latent ambiguities. If an ambiguity exists, extrinsic evidence is allowed to the extent necessary to clear up the ambiguity. The parole evidence rule's prohibition on the use of evidence to change or add to the contract remains intact.

CHAPTER 10: MODIFYING A CONTRACT

When and how can a contract be modified?

Most jurisdictions hold that the parties to a contract can modify the contract using the same formalities required to enforce the contract. This means that if the contract falls under the statute of frauds, any modification to the contract must also meet the statute of frauds requirements.

- *Example*: Tami enters into a contract to sell Anna a piece of equipment for $1,000. Since the contract is for the sale of goods of $500 or more, it falls under the statute of frauds and is required to be in writing. Later, Tami and Anna decide to modify the contract to include a warranty on the piece of equipment for a total of $1,100. Because the original contract is required to be in writing, the modification must be in writing. It does not matter that the subject of the modification (a warranty) would not necessarily be required to be in writing if done in a separate agreement.

- *Note*: Contract modifications are subject to the same defenses as the contract itself. They cannot have an illegal purpose, offend public policy, or be the result of misrepresentation, duress, fraud, etc.

Does a modification have to be supported by consideration?

Whether a modification must be supported by consideration depends on whether the contract is for the sale of goods or under the common law. The UCC calls for modification of the contract to have consideration to support the agreed upon modification. This rule is consistent with the general rule that a contract must be executed with the same level of formality as required in its formation. Under the common law in some jurisdictions, the contract must be supported by consideration unless an exception applies. Exceptions to the requirement for consideration include:

- Contracts for which exceptions to the requirement for consideration exist,

    - *Note*: Contracts that may not require consideration under the UCC include firm offers and agreements to pay a prior debt.

- Contracts where unforeseen difficulties cause both parties to seek modification and the modifications are fair and equitable under the circumstances, or

    - *Example*: Kurt operates a convenience store. Gerald supplies Kurt's store with merchandise. The area where Kurt's store is located is affected by major flooding from the local river. Because of the flooding, Kurt is not in a position to accept the current shipment of goods and Gerald has issues delivering those goods. This situation would permit the parties to modify the contract without additional consideration.

- Contracts where one party relies to her detriment on the enforceability of the modification.

    - *Example:* Karla enters into a contract to supply Connor with aluminum for manufacturing plant. Connor and Karla verbally agree to modify the agreement to supply Connor with a copper material. Karla purchases and begins refining the copper to meet Connor's needs. Connor later decides to continue working with aluminum and attempts to cancel the modification of the contract. The modification may not be enforceable because of the statute of frauds. Karla is upset because she has spent lots of time and money ramping up to produce copper material. She may be able to sue to enforce the modification based upon equitable principles (promissory estoppel).

Can parties waive the requirement that a modification be in writing?

Under the common law, most jurisdictions hold that contracts falling under the statute of frauds can only be modified in writing. A minority of jurisdictions take a case-by-case approach based upon principles of equity. The UCC requires that a modification be in writing if the original contract was in writing.

- *Example*: Kaitlyn enters into an agreement to purchase equipment with a value of $700 from Artis. The parties later seek to orally modify the contract to include additional equipment and to provide for a warranty that will last for 24 months. The new purchase price is $1,000. Later the parties get into a dispute and Artis does not want to warranty the equipment purchased by Kaitlyn. Kaitlyn sues alleging breach of contract. Artis defends on the grounds that the contract was not enforceable because it did not comply with the statute of frauds. The court would look to determine if the modification gave rise to a new contract. The contract is required to be written under the UCC and common law, as it is for more than $500 in goods (UCC) and the warranty period last more than 12 months (common law). Thus, Artis may prevail under the breach of contract claim regarding the warranty.

- *Note*: In either case, promissory estoppel may make a contract or modification that does not comply with the statute of frauds enforceable. Some written contracts that do not fall under the statute of frauds contain provisions stating that the contract cannot be modified orally. Jurisdictions are split on whether these provisions are enforceable.

Can an unenforceable attempt at modifying a contract waive the original contract terms?

Yes. If the parties attempt to modify a contract and the attempt is unenforceable for failure to comply with the statute of frauds or some other requirement, then that attempt can serve to waive certain other conditions in the contract.

- *Example*: Tom and Alice enter into a contract where Tom will sell Alice building supplies. The contract calls for Tom to give Alice notice if any shipment will be "more than two days late." The parties later attempt to modify the contract changing this time period to "5 days late." When a dispute later arises, the court holds that the modification is unenforceable because it does not meet the statute of frauds requirement. The court also holds that Tom's failure to give notice to Alice does not constitute a breach of the contract, as the parties expressly waived this provision when they attempted to modify the contract.

CHAPTER 11: WARRANTIES

What is a warranty in a contract?

A warranty is a representation by a party that something is true and will remain true until some point in time (generally the time of contract performance).

- *Example*: Tim owns a supply store and enters into a contract to sell Bernice a piece of equipment. Tim assures Bernice that the equipment is in good working order. Further, he warrants that the equipment will be in working order on the day that the sale is carried out.

Do warranties apply to goods and services?

Warranties generally exist in contracts for the sale of goods. The UCC provides for both express and implied warranties of goods sold by both merchants of those types of goods and non-merchants. Express warranties and implied warranties of merchantability, title, and fitness are discussed further below. In some jurisdictions, contracts for services carried out by a professional or someone holding themselves out as an expert include a warranty of workmanship. While a warranty is a contract term, the warranty of workmanship is generally engulfed in the standard of care owed by someone in carrying out an activity. As such, the warranty of workmanship gets subsumed in the tort of negligence.

- *Example*: In the above-referenced example, Tim is a merchant of those goods and makes an express warranty as to their functionality. If Tim were to include in the contract an obligation to install the equipment for Bernice, this would be a service. Some jurisdictions may find an implied warranty of workmanship. In most jurisdictions, however, a failure to properly install the equipment would simply lead to a breach of contract action (failure to complete duties - not a claim regarding a warranty) or a negligence action if someone is harmed by the faulty work.

- *Note*: A party who sells a good that does not meet an express or implied warranty thereby breaches the contract. A party who does not perform a service at a required level also breaches a contract. A professional service provider may be sued in tort for negligence (professional liability or malpractice).

What constitutes an express warranty by the seller of a good?

When a seller makes any assurances or statements of fact about the goods (including a description, drawing, model, etc.), then she expressly warrants that the goods will conform to those representations. It is not necessary to use the words "warranty" or "guarantee."

- *Example*: Edgar enters into a contract to sell a car to Wynona. Edgar states that the car does not leak oil. By stating this fact, Edgar makes an express warranty about the car. Because the contract is required to be in writing (the car is a good of $500 or more),

Wynona should ask Edgar to put it into the agreement. This will avoid issues of proving the express warranty and parole evidence issues.

- *Note*: A seller bragging about the quality of the goods (known as puffing) or stating a value for the goods is generally not a warranty. If, however, the individual making the brag is an expert in the field, then relying on that brag make constitute a warranty.

What is the implied warranty of title for goods?

In all sales of goods the seller warrants that she is transferring good title, that she has the right to transfer that title, and that the goods are not subject to outside interest (liens, encumbrances, security interests). If the seller is a merchant dealing in this type of goods, she warrants that the goods are free from claims of copyright, patent, or trademark infringement.

- *Example*: Keith enters into a contract to sell a piece of equipment to Julia. It is implied in the offer that Keith owns the equipment (or will own the equipment at the time of sale) and that the equipment is free of undisclosed liens or claims of ownership by third parties.

- *Note*: There is an exception if the goods are custom made at the direction of the buyer. In this case, the manufacturer does not warrant that the manufactured design does not violate third-party, intellectual property rights. The buyer requesting production bears the risk of any such infringement.

What is the implied warranty of merchantability for goods?

Merchants who sell goods warrant to any purchasers of the goods that they are merchantable. The word merchantability is a legal term that means the goods:

- Meet the standards under the contract and would meet industry standards for such a described good;
- Meet the quality standards of an average item of such description;
- Are fit for the ordinary and intended use of such goods;
- Are uniform in type and quality among all units subject to the transaction;
- Are appropriately packaged and labeled as to the packaged contents; and
- Meet any representations depicted on the item or packaging.

Generally, the implied warranty assures a purchaser that she is receiving the industry standard for the type and quality of goods that she bargained for under the contract.

What is the implied warranty of fitness for a particular purpose for goods?

This warranty applies to sales of goods by merchants and non-merchants. Unless expressly excluded in a contract, any seller of goods warrants that the goods are fit for the purposes for which they are sold if:

- the seller knows (or has reason to know) the purpose for which the goods are purchased, and
- the buyer relies on the seller's skill or judgment in selecting a suitable good.

- *Example*: Tom sells a piece of equipment to Jerry for use in his construction business. Tom knows of Jerry's intended use and assists him in picking out the specific equipment that he needs. Therefore, Tom impliedly warrants that the equipment sold is fit for Jerry's intended use. If the products are not fit for the intended use, then Tom breaches his warranty of fitness and Jerry may sue him.

Can a seller disclaim the implied warranties?

Yes. The standard for disclaiming an implied warranty depends upon the type of warranty. Generally, express language must be used to disclaim the implied warranty or title. In some instances, however, the implied warranty is disclaimed when the buyer knows or has reason to know that the seller is only attempting to sell her rights (whatever their extent) in the good. This often arises in transfers of inheritance rights in goods that are contested or uncertain.

As discussed above, the implied warranty of merchantability applies to goods sold by merchants. To disclaim the implied warranty of merchantability, the contract must expressly use the word "merchantability" in the disclaimer. The written disclaimer must also be conspicuous (such as capitalized or in bold) to the reader.

The disclaimer of the implied warranty of fitness must be in writing and conspicuous in the contract of sale. Unlike the warranty of merchantability, however, a general disclaimer stating that no warranties other than express warranties apply is generally sufficient to disclaim this warranty.

- *Example*: Wilt, a merchant, enters into a contract to sell Aaron equipment. Wilt is not certain about the quality of the equipment and all of the equipment is subject to a lien by a third-party lender. Aaron is willing to take the risk. In the contract, Wilt expressly states that there are no warranties and, specifically, that there is no warranty of merchantability. He also discloses the third-party lender's lien on the equipment. The contract states that the proceeds from sale will be used to pay off this lien at the time of purchase. The general disclaimer and specific disclaimer together are sufficient to disclaim the implied warranty of merchantability and fitness. The disclosure of the lien is sufficient to disclaim the implied warranty of title and also creates an obligation under the contract.

- *Note*: Implied warranties can arise or be further excluded by a course of dealing, course of performance, or trade usage.

What is a general disclaimer of warranties?

A general disclaimer attempts to disclaim all possible warranties in the sale of a good. Using specific words of disclaimer, such as "as is" or "with all faults," serves to disclaim the implied warranties of fitness and any other implied warranties (with the exception of the implied warrant of merchantability). These words must appear conspicuously in the contract. If the buyer is given the right to examine the goods prior to purchase or has refused to examine the goods, then there is no implied warranty for defects that should have been discovered on examination. The knowledge, skill, or experience of the buyer is considered in determining the extent of the warranties excluded.

- *Example*: Richard, a merchant, enters into a contract with Wilma to sell a shipment of notebooks. Richard conspicuously notes that the notebooks are sold, "as is." Wilma is very knowledgeable about notebooks and paper quality. She inspects a sample notebook and proceeds to order the shipment. Upon arrival, Wilma realizes that lead pencils do not write well on this type of paper. If she sues Richard under an implied warranty, her argument will have to be a breach of the implied warranty of merchantability. The "as is" notification expressly disclaims the warranty of fitness. Her claim may not prevail, however, as she should have discovered the defect in the quality of the paper upon careful inspection of the sample notebook.

- *Note*: The seller can further limit implied warranties by expressly disclosing any defects in the goods.

Can a general disclaimer of warranties disclaim an express warranty?

No. A general disclaimer cannot disclaim an express warranty. A general disclaimer and an express warranty will be construed consistently if reasonable to do so.

- *Example*: Carlos enters into a contract to sell an office printer to Jeffrey. Carlos expressly states in the contract that the printer will print in several colors and 50 pages per minute. At the bottom of the contract, Carlos expressly disclaims any warranties. When the printer fails to perform as stated, Jeffrey asks for a return of his money. When Carlos refuses to return the money, Jeffrey sues Carlos under a theory of breach of express warranty. Carlos will not be successful asserting that he disclaimed all warranties. A general disclaimer cannot disclaim an express warranty.

- *Note*: If a contract contains an express warranty and there is language expressly disclaiming the express warranty, then there is an ambiguity in the contract. The court will then consider outside evidence to determine the intent of the parties to the agreement.

CHAPTER 12: PERFORMANCE OF THE CONTRACT

What is the duty of performance?

Under a contract, each party has a duty to undertake (or refrain from undertaking) some activity. This is known as the "duty of performance." Basically, it is what each party seeks from the other party.

- *Example*: Clarence enters into a contract with Dina to wash her car. In this situation, Clarence's duty is to wash Dina's car. Dina's duty is to pay Clarence for washing his car.

- *Note*: In some situations, the duty to perform under the contract may only arise once certain conditions are in place. In the above example, the condition for Dina's performance is dependent upon Clarence performing his duty.

What does it mean to discharge one's duty of performance?

Discharge of one's duty means that the party has undertaken, completed, or forgone all of the activities required under the contract. She has no further duties thereunder.

- *Example*: In the situation above, once Clarence has washed Dina's car, he has discharged his duty under the contract.

- *Note*: Generally, parties either discharge their duty of performance (this includes being excused from the contract obligations) or are in breach of the contract.

What is complete, partial, and substantial performance?

Complete performance is where a party completes her entire obligation under the contract. Partial performance is a completion of some, but not all, of the material provisions under the contract. Partial performance is relevant for purposes of installment of divisible contracts. Partial performance may lead to breach of one portion of an installment contract, while leaving other portions of the contract enforceable. The same is true for divisible contracts. Substantial performance is completion of all material portions of the contract and failure to complete other non-material portions. Substantial performance generally avoids an action for breach of contract, but may give rise to an action for an equitable remedy, such as offset.

- *Example*: Frank enters into a contract with Diana to build her a home. Frank grades the land, lays the foundation, and begins framing the home. At this point, Frank has partially performed the contract. He has taken more than incidental steps toward completion of the contract. Frank continues construction under the contract and completes everything, except for painting the exterior of the house. Frank has likely substantially performed the contract. Substantial performance means all major obligations under the contract have been performed; there are, however, minor elements that have not been completed. While there is not complete performance due to the failure to paint the exterior, there is substantial performance because the entire house is built in accordance with the contract. Frank will have completed performance (complete performance), once the contract is completed in accordance with all terms of the contract.

- *Note*: If a party substantially performs, he is not liable for breach of contract. He may, however, be sued to offset the value of services paid for but not delivered.

What are "conditions of performance" in a contract?

A condition in a contract is when something must take place prior to or before a party has a duty to perform. That is, there is no obligation for the party to undertake any action, unless the condition occurs. Conditions are characterized as either express or implied and as either precedent or subsequent.

- *Example*: Eric enters into a contract with Mary stating, "if the Oakland Athletics win the American League championship series, I (Eric) will sell you (Mary) my season tickets to the World Series for face value." The Athletics winning the championship series is a condition to Eric's obligation to sell the tickets to Mary.

- *Note*: A condition can be an event, occurrence, non-occurrence, characteristic subject to discovery or revelation, etc.

What is an express and implied condition?

An express condition is any condition expressly stated by the parties as part of the contract. It can be oral or written. It simply has to be communicated, understood, and accepted by both parties as part of the contract. An implied condition, on the other hand, is not stated expressly as part of the contract; rather, it is implied from the language or nature of the contract.

- *Example:* Seller says that he will sell a vehicle to any customer for $1,000. Buyer accepts the offer, with the condition that the car pass a mechanic's inspection first. The Seller accepts the Buyer's terms and a contract is formed. An express condition to the Buyer's duty to perform is that the car pass a mechanic's inspection.

- *Note*: An implied condition under the UCC is that the customer make payment prior to the Seller delivering the item.

What is a condition precedent and condition subsequent?

A condition precedent is some event, condition, or occurrence that must take place before one party's duty of performance arises. A condition subsequent serves to excuse parties from their obligation under a previously formed contract upon some future event, condition, or occurrence.

- *Example*: "If the stock drops to $10 per share, I will purchase your 5 shares." This is an example of a condition precedent, because something must take place before the promisor is obligated under the contract.

- *Example*: "I will purchase your 5 shares for $10 at the end of the month. If the shares drop below an $8 market value, I do not have to purchase them." This is an example of a condition subsequent. I am obligated under the contract, but some future event, occurrence, or condition can excuse my duty of performance.

What are concurrent conditions?

Concurrent conditions are two or more conditions that must take place or both parties are excused from the contract. In the examples above, each party has a duty to perform. The condition affects (and possibly excuses) one party's duty to perform. The other party maintains the duty to perform until the other party elects to be excused from their duty. A concurrent condition simultaneously excuses both parties' duty to perform.

- *Example*: In a contract for Will to sell Grace his car, the contract requires that the car pass inspection and that Grace (the buyer) be able to obtain financing for the purchase. If either of these concurrent conditions fails, then both parties are free from their duties to buy and sell the car.

What is fulfillment of a condition?

A condition must take place (or not occur) either naturally or as a result of the parties' efforts. Fulfillment is the occurrence (or non-occurrence) that takes place and gives rise to a party's duty to perform.

- *Example*: In the above example of Will and Grace, the fulfillment of the conditions is the car passing the mechanic's inspection and Grace finding financing for the purchase.

What is strict fulfillment of a condition?

Certain conditions must be completely fulfilled (strictly fulfilled) before a duty of performance arises. All express conditions are subject to strict fulfillment. In most jurisdictions, any conditions implied from the course of performance, course of dealing, or from a trade usage must also be strictly fulfilled.

- *Example*: In the example of Will and Grace, if the car passes 9 of 10 points on the mechanic's inspection, it may not be in strict fulfillment of the condition. If the contract calls for the car to pass every element of the mechanic's inspection, substantial passage is not sufficient. Even if the failed element is easily corrected, the condition is still not fulfilled.
- *Note*: A condition may be fulfilled at any time prior to expiration of the period allocated for fulfillment.

What is substantial fulfillment of a condition?

Substantial performance is the completion of the major aspects of an obligation. Unlike complete performance, however, substantial performance falls short of complete and total fulfillment of an obligation. Often a court (generally a court applying equity or fairness principles) will impose a condition on the court-ordered transaction between two parties in order to prevent an injustice under an existing contract. Such a condition will be subject to substantial performance or substantial fulfillment. If the condition is substantially filled, then the contract will remain in full force and effect.

- *Example*: Alex enters into a contract with Jennifer for the sale of equipment. Pursuant to the contract, Jennifer makes numerous representations. When Alex receives the equipment, it is not functioning as expected. Jennifer refuses to accept return of the equipment and retains Alex's money. Alex sues Jennifer for misrepresentation in the sale of the equipment. The court orders Alex to return the property to Jennifer in the exact condition in which it was delivered. Once the equipment is returned, Jennifer must return the purchase funds to Alex. Alex returning the equipment to Jennifer as specified is a condition to Jennifer's returning the purchase price to Alex.

Are there any excuses that make a contract enforceable when a condition is not fulfilled?

Yes. There are certain circumstances where a condition will be excused and the parties will be subject to a duty to perform.

- Wrongful interruption by one party prevents the occurrence of a condition.

    - *Example*: Zora enters into a contract with Sam to sell him equipment. Zora refuses to accept payment from Sam when payment is due. Because payment is a condition precedent to Zora delivering the goods, it would appear that a condition precedent has failed. Since Zora has caused the failure of the condition (payment by Sam), she cannot rely on the failure of the condition to defend her failure to perform.

    - *Note*: This exception is based upon principles of equity. It would not be fair to allow a party to interrupt a contract by her own actions. This is similar to the reasoning behind why illusory promises are insufficient as consideration.

- Waiver of the condition by the parties will excuse the condition.

    - *Example*: Neil enters into a contract with Judith to sell her a vehicle so long as the vehicle passes a mechanic's inspection. When the car fails the inspection, Judith states that she is willing to purchase the car anyway and provides Neil the purchase money. Since the parties continue to perform following the failure of the condition, it will be deemed waived.

    - *Note*: In some case, the conduct of the parties may constitute a waiver. In any event, a waiver by one party can be withdrawn if the other party has not relied on the waiver to her detriment.

- If performance of a non-material condition would cause a disproportionate loss to one party under the contract or the performance of the condition becomes impossible.

    - *Example*: Gale enters into a contract with Jackie to supply cement for her construction business. Selling the cement is contingent upon Jackie getting a purchase order to Gale at least 14 days prior to the shipment date. Jackie and Gale carry on operations successfully for some time. Gale routinely sells the cement without receiving the purchase order 14 days in advance of shipping. Gale and Jackie begin having disagreements. In the middle of a large job, Jackie sends the purchase order to Gale approximately 13 days prior to the requested shipment date. Gale refuses to sell the cement due to the failure of the condition. If Jackie will suffer a disproportionate detriment due to the failure of the condition, the court may ignore the failure of the condition in evaluating whether Gale breached the contract.

    - *Note*: If performance of the condition is a material part of the bargain, then impossibility or disproportionate loss is not an excuse.

- If the actions or consent of a third-party to a contract is a condition under the agreement, the unjustified or unreasonable failure of the third-party to perform or consent will excuse the condition if certain requirements are met.

    - *Example*: Neil enters into a contract with Judith to sell her a vehicle if the vehicle passes a mechanic's inspection. The mechanic completes part of the inspection, but refuses to complete the work in a timely manner. He also refuses to complete an inspection report, as required in the contract. Because of the mechanic's failure or refusal to complete his inspection (a condition under the contract), the court may excuse this condition in enforcing a contract or determining whether a breach has occurred.

    - *Note*: This is particularly important in contracts that require subjective evaluations and opinions by third parties.

What standards apply if a contract makes approval by a third party an express condition in the contract?

A condition precedent or subsequent based upon the subjective determinations or approval of a third party is generally enforceable. The third party's death or incapacity will not interrupt this condition. As discussed above, if the third party acts unreasonably in failing to act or withholding their approval, it will not excuse the condition unless the failure of the condition will result in a loss (or forfeiture) by the other party. If a loss or forfeiture would occur, then the court will look to the nature of the third-parties obligation under the condition. If the condition is expressly dependent on a third party's subjective beliefs, interpretations, or taste, then a failure to give approval will not excuse the condition. If, however, the third-party's duty is functional (such as carrying out a routine activity) or is not based upon some professional certification, qualification, or opinion, then a failure to undertake that activity may excuse the condition.

- *Example*: In the situation of Neil and Judith, the mechanic withheld his physical report as to whether the vehicle meets prescribed mechanical standards. In such a case, the failure to perform the inspection and create the report will excuse the condition. As such, Neil cannot refuse to sell the car due to the absence of a mechanic's report. Since the condition is in place to protect Judith, she can refuse to purchase the vehicle without the inspection report.

- *Example*: In the above example, if the contract requires that the mechanic give his affirmative opinion that the vehicle is a certain quality and the mechanic refuses, a failure to do so will likely not excuse the condition. In this case, the mechanic is not simply failing to undertake his duties; rather, he knowingly withholds a favorable opinion that is required or is a condition to the duties under the contract arising. In any event, Neil's duty to sell and Judith's duty to purchase the vehicle will not arise and they are excused from the contract.

What if a condition to a duty to perform is based upon one party's approval of a situation?

Courts generally enforce provisions where a condition to a party's duty to perform is based on her subjective approval of the other party's performance. If the failure of the condition will result in a loss to the other party, the court will examine the context of the condition. If the condition is specifically based on the other parties taste or preference, the court will uphold it if the other party is honestly dissatisfied. If the condition is based upon a general task or function by the approving party, the court will look to make certain it is not unreasonably withheld.

- *Example*: Adam contracts with Dan to paint a modern art piece to hang on his wall. The contract make's Adam's duty to pay Dan contingent upon Adam's approval of the art piece. When Dan presents the finished piece to Adam, Adam is not pleased with the work and refuses to pay for the art. If Dan sues Adam for payment, the court will likely hold that no breach has occurred. Adam's duty to pay Dan only arises upon a condition being satisfied (Dan approving the painting).

- *Example*: In the above situation, the condition on performance is that Adam must transfer funds from his saving account to pay Dan. If Adam simply refuses to move the money, this is a manual failure on the part of Adam. This condition will not excuse Adam's duty to pay Dan for his work.

- *Note*: If the non-performing party is unjustly enriched at the expense of the performing party, the performing party may be entitled to compensation based upon principles of unjust enrichment.

What events or conditions discharge a party's contractual duties to perform?

As discussed above, a party is discharged from her duty to perform under the contract upon performance (either complete or substantial) of the contract. Also, a failure of a condition will excuse and individual's performance. Other manners of excusing or discharging one's duty under a contract include:

- rescission of the contract by the parties;
- substitution of the contract;
- reaching an accord and satisfaction;
- novation of the agreement;
- voiding a voidable contract;
- the contract purpose becoming illegal;
- a bankruptcy court staying performance of a contract;
- breach of contract by the other party;
- Impossibility or impracticability; or
- frustration of the contract's purpose.

Each of these manners of discharging performance is discussed below.

What is rescission of a contract?

This is where both parties mutually agree to undo (or rescind) a contract that has not been completely performed. Jurisdictions are split on the level of formality required for rescission. If neither party has begun performance, new consideration is not required to rescind the contract. If either party has taken significant steps toward performance, then new consideration is required. Under the common law, many jurisdictions do not require that a rescission be in writing, even if the original contract was in writing. The UCC, however, requires that the rescission of any contract under the statute of frauds also be in writing if the contract requires written modifications or rescissions. This rule coincides with the rule regarding modification of a contract.

- *Example*: Francis enters into a contract with Tommy to paint his house. She has not paid Tommy and he has not begun performance. The parties may rescind the agreement without new consideration or the need for a writing. If, however, Tommy has begun performance, Francis may have to enter into a new agreement with Tommy in order to rescind the original agreement. The new agreement, like any contract, will require some form of new consideration (such as paying a higher rate for the services already performed). The new agreement likely does not have to be in writing, even if the original contract was in writing.

- *Note*: Rescission may not be available if it affects the rights vested in a third party.

What is an accord and satisfaction?

An accord and satisfaction is an agreement between the parties. It states that a given level of performance by either or both parties (that is less than complete performance of the contract) is sufficient to satisfy that party's obligation under the agreement.

- *Example*: Jane paints Eric's house under an agreement where Eric will pay her $1,000 upon completion. Eric does not believe the job is complete because Jane should have put two coats of paint. Jane refuses to paint another coat of paint. Eric refuses to pay $1,000 for the services. The parties get tired of arguing and enter into an accord and satisfaction, whereby Eric will pay Jane $700 for the paint job. The accord and satisfaction excuses the obligations under the original contract.

What is a substitute contract?

The parties enter into a completely new contract that supersedes and replaces the old contract. After the new contract is executed, the old contract is no longer enforceable and the duties owed thereunder are excused.

- *Example*: Carlos enters into a contract with Jan to build him a fence. Carlos later approaches Jan and offers to pay her an additional sum to also build him a new deck for his house. Jan and Carlos execute a new agreement that expressly supersedes the original agreement. This substitute contract will excuse any duties previously required under the old contract.
- *Note*: An accord and satisfaction settles an issue between the parties where one or both parties fail to completely perform. A substitute contract simply disregards and replaces the old contract.

What is novation?

Novation is where one party transfers her rights or obligations to another party. The non-transferring party then agrees to substitute the other party and to excuse the transferring party's duties under the contract. To affect this change, the non-transferring party and the new party enter into an agreement obligating her to the contract and excusing the transferring party.

- *Example*: Diane and Ervin enter into a contract for the sale of goods. Diane attempts to transfer her obligation to supply the goods under the contract to Alfred. Diane wishes to be excused from the contract. If Alfred and Ervin enter into a new agreement that expressly adopts the agreement between Diane and Ervin, then the original agreement is extinguished. The formation of the new contract (or novation) will control the relationship between and Alfred and Ervin.

What is a release?

A release is an expression by one party (the party owed a duty of performance) that the other party does not have to perform their obligation. That is, the party is released from her obligation under the agreement.

- *Example*: Mike enters into a contract to sell his car to Julian. Later, Julian tells Mike that he does not wish to purchase the car. Mike, not upset at Julian, releases Julian from the contract. Since the contract was for the sale of a good of $500 or more, both the contract and Mike's release of Julian must be in writing.

What is impossibility of performance?

Impossibility of performance is when the conditions surrounding a contract make it impossible for a party to perform her obligation. Impossibility will excuse a party's performance where the circumstances are not the fault or under the control of the non-performing party and the party did not expressly or impliedly accept or bear the risk of performance becoming impossible.

- *Example*: Rachel enters into a contract to supply Persian rugs for sale at Winston's rug supply. Rachel sources the rugs from Iran and sells them in the United States. Due to deteriorating relations between Iran and the U.S., the U.S. Government places an embargo on all goods from Iran. This embargo makes it illegal for Rachel to sell the Persian rugs. In this case, Rachel would be excused from the contract under the doctrine of impossibility of performance. The illegality of selling the rugs means that it is legally impossible for Rachel to perform and it is at no fault of her own.

- *Note*: Events that make a contract impossible include:

    - Illegality of the subject matter;

        - *Note*: The above example of Rachel and Winston is an example of the subject matter of the agreement becoming illegal.

    - The subject of the contract (property) is destroyed;

        - *Example:* Marshal agrees to sell a specific piece of equipment to Linda. The piece of equipment is destroyed before Marshal can deliver it. Because it was a specific piece of equipment that is not readily replaced, this would render performance of the contract impossible.

    - One of the parties to the contract dies or becomes physically or mentally disabled;

        - *Note:* If a party is rendered physically or mentally unable to perform the contract, it is excused. If, however, the individual recovers within the time period allowed by the contract or within a reasonable time, the contract may still be enforceable.

    - Natural forces interrupt the contract (tornado, earthquake, severe storms, flooding, etc.);

        - *Example:* A tornado destroys the methods of shipping to a town. As such, it becomes impossible to make delivers of goods to local stores. The

- Performance would cause substantial risk of physical harm to one party.

  - *Example*: Kyle agrees to paint Julia's house this weekend. The wind is blowing extremely hard all weekend. The danger to Kyle in painting the house in this heavy wind makes performance of the contract unduly risky

The justification for the above exemptions regards the unexpected nature of the interruption in contractual performance. The interruption is not specifically attributable to any party and, therefore, should not unduly burden either of the parties.

What is impracticability?

Impracticability is where performance of a contract by a party has become unfeasibly difficult or costly to perform. The difference between impracticability and impossibility is that impracticability is still physically possible – it simply results in a substantial hardship to the performing party. Impracticability will excuse performance where the excused party did not have control over (or was not at fault for) the condition that made performance impracticable. Further, the excused party must not have expressly or impliedly assumed the risk of the duties becoming impracticable.

- *Example*: Claire enters into a contract with Phil to supply him with live crabs for his restaurant. Claire and Phil settle on a price that reflects the risk of market conditions. The following month, the local government levies a large tax on local seafood. The tax causes Claire to suffer a substantial loss on every bushel of crabs sold at the pre-negotiated price. This may be a case where Claire is excused from the contract under a theory of impracticability. The increase in taxes is an unforeseen event that was outside of Claire's control. She will suffer a huge detriment if not relieved from the contract.

- *Note*: Generally, impracticability is only found in extreme circumstances. Such instances include major price swings due to government action or international relations. In any event, impracticability generally requires the relieved party to suffer some form of unreasonable burden, risk, or expense.

What is supervening frustration of purpose?

This is when circumstances arise that fundamentally frustrate a party's reason or purpose for entering a contract. The doctrine is similar to impracticability, but it does not relate to a party's hardship; rather it focuses on her expectation and purpose in entering the agreement. For a frustrating circumstance to relieve or excuse an obligation under a contract, the party cannot have assumed the risk of the circumstance (in the contract), be at fault for the occurrence or the non-occurrence of the event or circumstance, and the occurrence or non-occurrence must have been a basic assumption on which the contract was made.

- *Note:* Suffering an economic loss is not a frustration of purpose.

- *Example*: John signs up for piano playing lessons from Tara. John suffers a horrible accident that causes him to lose dexterity in his hands. This is a frustration of purpose that was unforeseeable and substantially frustrates the purpose of learning to play the piano. As such, John will be excused from performance of the contract.

CHAPTER 13: BREACH OF CONTRACT

What is breach of contract?

As previously stated, if any party fails to perform (completely or substantially) or fails to find an excuse to the obligations in the contract, then there is a breach. A breach may include inaction, incomplete action, or the wrong action by the party with a duty to perform.

- *Example*: Perry enters into a bilateral contract with Vince to wash his car. Time passes and Perry never washes Vince's car. After a reasonable time (or the period stated in the contract), Perry has breached his contract with Vince. Even if Vince never takes action to enforce the agreement, Perry is still in breach. Vince has not breached, as Perry's failure to fulfill a condition (wash the car) means that Vince's duty to perform (pay Perry) never arose.

- *Note*: As demonstrated above, doing nothing when there is an obligation to act is a breach. Likewise, acting when there is an obligation not to act is also a breach.

What is a material breach of a contract?

When a party fails to perform some material aspect of a contract (i.e., does not substantially perform) there is a breach. In such a case, the non-breaching party may halt performance and sue for damages under the contract.

- *Example*: Thomas hires Danny to illustrate the children's book he has written. Thomas agrees to pay Danny in installments as he completes sections of the book. Thomas fails to pay Danny the second installment. This is a material breach and Danny may stop work on the book and sue for damages.

- *Note*: If a party substantially performs, the other party may still sue for any loss of value due to the incomplete performance.

Courts employ a number of factors to determine whether the failure to perform any part of a contract is material and therefore a breach. These factors include:

- Whether the non-breaching party will suffer a detriment (or forgo a benefit);
- Whether the non-breaching party can be adequately compensated for the other party's failure to completely perform (such as through offset);
- Whether the party breaching party is willing, able, or likely to cure the breach; and
- Whether the breaching party did so intentionally (acted in bad faith) or innocently (acted in good faith).

If a party fails to perform only a non-material aspect of the contract, then she has substantially performed the contract, and there is no breach.

What are a party's rights to cure a material breach?

Under the common law (transactions not involving the sale of goods), jurisdictions are split as to whether a party who commits a material breach of contract can cure that breach. Some jurisdictions allow the party to cure the breach as long as the period for performance has not lapsed. Other jurisdictions only allow a party to cure if the contract expressly grants that right. Under the UCC (transactions involving the sale of goods), the ability of a seller to cure a material breach of contract depends on the timing of the transaction. If the period for performance has not lapsed, then the breaching party may generally cure. If the contract is silent regarding a time period, then the breaching party may cure in a reasonable period of time.

- *Example*: Samantha enters into a contract to sell equipment to Kate. The contract calls for Samantha to deliver the equipment before the end of the week. On Monday, Samantha supplies a piece of equipment that is not functioning properly. Kate notifies Samantha on Tuesday. Samantha will likely have until the end of the week to replace the faulty equipment with equipment functioning appropriately.

What does it mean to "tender performance"?

Tendering performance simply means to offer or attempt to perform one's obligations under a contract. It is the tender of one party's performance that generally triggers another party's duty to perform.

- *Example*: Mabel enters into a contract with Steven to purchase supplies. She attempts to make payment to Steven. This is tendering performance. Upon a reasonable tender of performance by Mabel, Steven now has the obligation to deliver those supplies. If Steven, through his own fault, does not accept the tender of performance from Mabel (payment), he still has a duty to deliver the supplies. At that point, he simply has the right to collect the payment from Mabel.

What is a non-conforming tender of goods?

Under the UCC, the "perfect tender rule" states that, in a contract for the sale of goods, if the goods fail to conform exactly to the specifications of the contract, the buyer may reject the goods. Any failure to deliver goods in the time, manner, and quality described under the contract is a non-conforming tender. Basically, it is an attempt at performance of the contractual obligations that falls short.

- *Example*: In the case of Mabel and Steven, suppose Steven either delivers supplies that do not meet the requirements specified in the contract, delivers the goods at the wrong time, or delivers the goods to the wrong location. Any of these situations constitute a non-conforming tender of performance. In any of these situations, Mabel has the right to reject the tender of performance. This means that her duty to pay for the goods does not arise. If Mabel accepts the non-conforming tender (e.g., retains the goods delivered at the wrong time), then she will have a duty to perform (pay for the goods).

What are the rights of a party to reject a non-conforming tender of goods?

Before or within a reasonable time after receipt of non-conforming goods, the recipient may reject those goods. The recipient must notify the seller of the goods. If she does so, then she has not accepted the goods. If, however, the Buyer accepts the goods, then she generally cannot reject the tender (but she may be able to revoke acceptance in certain circumstances). Her sole remedy will be to sue for breach of contract.

- *Example*: In the case of Mabel and Steven, if Steven delivers non-conforming goods, Mabel must reject the goods within a reasonable time of receipt. This generally means that she must notify Steven that she is rejecting the non-conforming goods. If she fails to reject the non-conforming goods, she is deemed to have accepted them.

What happens if there is a defective tender in a single shipment under an installment contract?

If a contract is for the one-time delivery of goods, then the buyer who receives a defective tender may reject the delivery, accept the delivery (and sue for damages), or accept any part of the delivery and reject the rest. As previously discussed, this is known as the "perfect tender" rule. The buyer can reject the whole lot for deficiencies in a portion of the goods tendered. This rule is limited by the Buyer's obligation of good faith.

If the tender is part of an installment contract, the Buyer can only reject the tender of an installment if the non-conformity of goods substantially impairs that installment. Substantial impairment may pertain to the quality of the goods, timing of tender, quantity, etc. The non-conforming party will generally have the opportunity to cure the deficient tender. The buyer must reasonably cooperate with the attempt to cure through the offset of price, delivery of conforming goods, etc. If the party fails to cure, then this will give rise to a breach of contract.

- *Example*: Faith enters into a contract with Lawrence to supply steel for a construction project. Faith provides the first shipment and Lawrence accepts it. The second shipment, however, contains a different type of steel than the type ordered (a non-conforming good). Lawrence rejects the shipment and buys the needed steel for this shipment elsewhere. When it comes time for the third shipment, Faith ships the correct product. Lawrence may either accept the third shipment or reject it. The second shipment fails the perfect tender rule. Since it was non-conforming, Lawrence may cancel the entire contract, accept the non-conforming goods, or accept the 1st and 3rd shipments and reject the rest. In any scenario, Lawrence may sue for any damages suffered as a result of the breach of contract.

- *Note*: Under certain conditions, the buyer may be able to cure the deficiency or non-conforming tender. This is particularly true if the time for performance has not yet run.

When are goods deemed accepted and, thus, rejecting the tender offer is not possible?

Generally acceptance occurs when:

- the good has been delivered to the recipient,
- the recipient has a reasonable time to inspect the goods, and
- either:
    - The goods conform to the contract,
    - The recipient indicates that he will retain the goods even though they are non-conforming,
    - The recipient fails to effectively reject the goods, or
    - The recipient uses the goods in a way that is inconsistent with the seller's ownership of the goods (e.g., places the goods in service or sells them).

Can a party revoke the acceptance of goods?

Yes. As previously stated, a party in receipt of non-conforming goods can reject the shipment. If the party has already accepted the shipment, he can reject the goods within a reasonable time of receipt if the defective nature of the goods was not apparent at the time of receipt. This allows the party sufficient time to identify the non-conformity. The buyer may also revoke acceptance after receipt if he accepted the shipment under the assumption that the other party would cure the defective shipment. The recipient cannot revoke the goods if he should have discovered the defect within a reasonable time, but fails to do so. This often happens after the recipient uses the goods for a period or otherwise substantially changes the condition of the goods (such as incorporating them into the manufacturing process). In any event, the recipient must notify the other party immediately upon discovery of the defect.

- *Example*: Curtis enters into a contract with Lynn to supply parts for inclusion in production items that Lynn manufactures. If Curtis delivers faulty parts, Lynn can reject them at the time of receipt. If the defects in the parts are not obvious, then Lynn has a reasonable time to discover the defects and then to revoke acceptance of the shipment. If Lynn recognizes the defect immediately, he can retain the goods under the assumption that Curtis will replace the parts or otherwise cure the defect. If Curtis fails to cure the defect, then Lynn can revoke acceptance of the shipment. If Lynn recognizes the defect and is lackadaisical about notifying Curtis, he cannot revoke acceptance of the goods outside of a reasonable time period. If Lynn begins using the goods in the manufacturing process and substantially changes the condition of the goods, he cannot later revoke the goods. In this case, he would simply have to sue for breach and any damages suffered as a result of the breach.

What are a seller's rights to cure a non-conforming delivery or tender of goods?

A seller of goods is generally entitled to cure a defective tender of non-conforming goods if:

- the time for performance (delivery) has not expired,
- the seller notifies the buyer of the intention to cure within a timely manner, and
- the seller makes a conforming delivery within the applicable time period.
- *Example:* In the case of Curtis and Lynn, Curtis delivers faulty parts to Lynn. Lynn immediately notifies Curtis of the defective goods. If the time period specified for when Lynn needs the goods has not expired, Curtis may notify Lynn of his intention to supply conforming goods within the contract period. If Curtis indeed ships conforming goods within the contract period, then there is no breach of contract. Lynn must make the defective goods available for Curtis to reclaim.

The seller may have additional time to cure (beyond the contract period) if she notifies the buyer within a reasonable period and she has a reasonable belief that the non-conforming goods would be acceptable with a money allowance for any non-conformity.

- *Example*: Continuing with the case of Curtis and Lynn, suppose Curtis delivered the non-conforming goods and notified Lynn that they were not exactly as specified in the contract. He states that the variation is minor and that he will offset the difference in value from the price. If he reasonably believes that this will be acceptable, he may be afforded additional time under the contract to ship the conforming goods if Lynn rejects both the non-conforming goods and setoff offer.

What is anticipatory repudiation?

Anticipatory repudiation is the ability to repudiate a contract (reject one's obligation under a contract) based upon the other party's conduct. Anticipatory repudiation begins with any words or actions by a party that reasonably make the other party believe that she is going to breach the contract. Any such words or actions allow the other party to repudiate (reject or break away from) the contract in anticipation of the other party's breach.

- *Example*: Jason enters into an agreement to paint Wyatt's home by the end of the week. Wyatt really needs the house painted quickly to be ready for an upcoming event he is hosting. The next day Jason accepts a contract to paint a very large home on the other side of town. This will obviously take a long time and will take up the majority of Jason's time. Wyatt becomes aware of this and notifies Jason that he is canceling or repudiating the contract. He wants to free himself up to hire another painter. He tells Jason that he is repudiating the agreement because he anticipates that Jason will not be able to do a good job on his home if he does not devote his full time to the effort. If Jason later sues Wyatt for canceling the contract, Wyatt's defense will be anticipatory repudiation. He cancelled the contract before Jason had the opportunity to breach it.

How does a party indicate that she is going to breach the contract and allow the other party the right of anticipatory repudiation?

A party can make a statement indicating that she intends to breach the contract. She can engage in conduct that makes it extremely unlikely that she will be able to perform the contract without significant hardship or loss. Further, one party may seek assurance of performance based upon some reasonable evidence or belief that the other party will not perform. If the other party fails to respond to the request, then it can give rise to anticipatory repudiation.

- *Example*: In the case of Jason and Wyatt, Jason acted in a way that was inconsistent with his intention or ability to fulfill the contract. If Wyatt has sought assurance from Jason that he would perform, then Jason would have to show that he would be able to complete the required work. This may have included an explanation that Jason's work crew would work on the other project, while Jason worked on Wyatt's home. If Jason fails to provide some form of assurance, Wyatt would be justified in repudiating the contract.

What is a party's right to demand assurances of performance from another party?

Under common law and the UCC, when a party has reasonable grounds to believe that the other party will fail to perform their obligations under the agreement, she can demand an assurance of performance from the other party. Under the UCC, this demand must be in writing. If reasonable, the demanding party can suspend her performance until the other party provides the necessary assurances. If a party fails to provide the requested assurances within a reasonable time, this may justify repudiation of the contract.

- *Example*: In the case of Jason and Wyatt, Wyatt's request for assurances from Jason is under the common law and does not have to be in writing. Wyatt can validly withhold payment until he receives assurances of performance from Jason.

What are the rights of a party who anticipatorily repudiates a contract?

Under the common law, the repudiating party is discharged under the contract and she can sue the breaching party for damages. If a contract is for the sale of goods, the party can suspend performance, notify the other party, and await performance by that party. After a reasonable period of time, the aggrieved party can sue for breach.

- *Example*: In the case of Jason and Wyatt, Wyatt may sue Jason for any damages he incurred because of Jason's breach. If Wyatt hires another painter of equal qualifications but who is more expensive, he may be able to sue Jason for the difference between the contract price and the replacement painter's price.

Can a party who repudiates the contract undo or withdraw her repudiation?

A party who repudiates a contract based on the other party's anticipated breach may retract or withdraw her repudiation at any time before the other party's performance is due, unless the other party has cancelled the contract, materially changed her position, or otherwise accept the repudiation as final. In a contract for the sale of goods, the time when the contract is due would be the time of delivery of the goods or the next installment. In an installment contract falling under the common law, the repudiation can be withdrawn even after the time when the party's performance is due.

- *Example*: In the case of Jason and Wyatt, Wyatt may withdraw his repudiation at any time prior to the end of the week, when services are due. If Jason acknowledges the repudiation, however, it cannot be withdrawn. Likewise, if Jason relies on the repudiation and continues to book or work on other painting jobs, the repudiation is final as it would likely detriment him to allow the repudiation to be withdrawn.

What are the general defenses to a breach of contract?

All of the previously discussed elements of a valid or enforceable contract can serve as a defense to an allegation of breach of contract. As a recap, the general defenses are summarized as follows:

- Lack of Consideration - If a purported agreement lacks an exchange of consideration between the parties, it is not valid.

- Failure of Statute of Frauds - If a contract is subject to and fails to meet the requirements of the statute of frauds, it may be unenforceable.

- Mutual Mistake of Fact - Recall that a contract requires a meeting of the minds between the parties. Mutual mistake disrupts that meeting of the minds and thereby makes the contract voidable by either party.

- Lack of Mental Capacity - If a party lacks mental capacity at the time of entering into the contract or during the term of the contract, it could render the contract voidable by that party.

- Fraud, Duress, Misrepresentation - Fraud, Duress, or Misrepresentation are defenses to an alleged breach of contract.

- Unconscionable - An unconscionable contract is voidable as a matter of public policy.

- Impossibility or Impracticability - An impossible or impracticable contract either cannot be accomplished or would unduly burden one party as a result of an unexpected occurrence that was not the fault of either party.

- Equitable Principles - Principles of fairness and justice may give rise to a defense to a breach of contract.

All of the above defenses are subject to the exceptions previously mentioned in the explanation of that particular contract element.

CHAPTER 14: REMEDIES FOR BREACH OF CONTRACT

What are a seller's rights in the event of breach by a buyer?

A breach by one party relieves the non-breaching party from her duty of performance under the contract. In the case of a breach by a buyer, the buyer has failed to make payment in accordance with the terms of the agreement. A non-breaching seller's options include:

- withholding or stopping delivery of goods,
- reclaiming goods delivered, and
- reselling the goods and recovering damages for the breach.

- *Example*: Dale enters into a contract to sell goods to Gwen. Gwen fails to pay for the goods before shipment. Dale, expecting payment to arrive, ships the goods. Gwen never pays for the goods. In this case, Dale will have the right to reclaim the goods shipped to Gwen and to resell them.

- *Note*: A seller of goods is not allowed to breach the peace (e.g., get into a physical altercation) in the process of reclaiming goods. If a breach of peace would arise, the seller is forced to use legal channels (i.e., the court system) to reclaim the goods.

What are the buyer's rights in the event of breach by a seller?

If the Seller breaches the contract before the buyer renders payment, the general rights of the buyer include:

- Purchasing replacement goods (known as "cover") and seeking damages for the difference in the cost of the replacement goods; or

    - *Example*: Robert agrees to sell grant 100 bags of cement for his construction project at $10 per bag. Two days prior to the commencement of construction, Robert notifies grant that he cannot supply the cement. Grant must search for an immediate supplier and is forced to pay $15 per bag. Purchasing the replacement cement qualifies as cover. Grant may be able to sue Robert for $500, his loses in purchasing the replacement cement.

- Seeking any legal or equitable remedies available for the breach.

    - *Example*: In the above example, if Grant is not able to find replacement cement to start construction, he may be able to sue Robert for any damages he incurred as a result of the breach.

A buyer generally must make payment for goods before the seller has the duty to ship those goods. As such, a breach by a seller generally happens after the buyer has paid for goods. Remedies available to a buyer for a seller's breach include:

- Recovering the price paid for the goods,
- Withholding any additional payments due,
- Deducting any damages suffered by the breach from any payments due, and
- Seeking any legal or equitable remedies available for the breach (such as suing for damages or specific performance).

- *Example*: Robert enters into a contract to sell equipment to Sam. The contract requires Sam to pay 1/2 of the price up front and 1/2 of the price upon receipt of the equipment. Sam pays the 1/2 price up front, but he never receives the equipment. Sam will be able to withhold any further payment and seek a return of the initial payment. If Robert fails to return the initial payment, Sam may sue Robert to recoup the funds. If Sam suffered other damages as a result of Robert's failure to perform (consequential damages), he may be able to sue Robert to recover of those loses.

What remedies are available to a party for breach of contract?

The remedies available to the non-breaching party vary with the specifics of the contract. Several potential types of damages are available, including compensatory damages, liquidated damages, nominal damages, and (rarely) punitive damages. Other remedies available to the non-breaching party are based in equity and include, restitution, specific performance, rescission of the contract, or reformation of the contract. Each of these remedies is discussed below.

What are compensatory damages?

Compensatory damages serve to compensate a non-breaching party for damages suffered due the breach of contract. Compensatory damages are broken down into expectation damages and consequential damages.

What are expectation damages?

These are court-awarded damages to put the plaintiff in the same position as if the contract had been performed. They include lost profits on the contract and the cost of getting substitute performance.

- *Example*: Damian contracts Josh to wash his car in exchange for $20. Josh fails to wash his car as set forth in the agreement. Damian is forced to pay a third party to wash the car. The best price that Damian can find for someone of equal talent to Josh is $25. Because Damian had to pay more for replacement services, he suffered damages in the amount of $5. Damian lost the benefit of the bargain with Josh. As such, Damian can sue Josh to recover the loss of benefit sustained ($5).

What are consequential damages?

These are court-awarded damages arising from losses that the parties knew would result from breach of the contract. These are damages that flow from or are a natural consequence of the breach of contract, but are not derived from the actual contract.

- *Example*: In the case of Damian and Josh, Damian suffered expectation damages by having to hire another person to wash his car. Assume that Damian needed a professional to wash his car to prevent the dirt on the car from causing permanent damage to his paint. By the time he could hire a trained third party to wash the car, he had already suffered damages to his paint. As a result, Damian had to have his car repainted to restore it to its former condition. The damage suffered to the paint was caused by Josh's failure to wash the car. While this was not an expectation damage of the contract, it was a damage that flowed naturally from the breach. It was reasonably foreseeable that this type of damage could arise. As such, Damian can sue Josh for the consequential damages suffered due to his failure to wash the car.

What are liquidated damages?

Where real damages for breach of contract are likely to be uncertain, parties sometimes specify in the contract what the damages should be in the event of breach. These damages must adequately represent the actual loss suffered by the party as a result of the breach. Courts will not enforce these "liquidated" damages if they seem to penalize the defendant instead of merely compensating the plaintiff for uncertain losses. Under common law, the reasonableness of stipulated damages must reflect:

- the anticipated or actual harm caused by the breach; and
- the difficulties of proof of loss.

- *Example*: Carla enters into a contract hiring Toby to perform at a major event that she is hosting. In the contract, Toby negotiates a liquidated damages clause. While Toby is being paid $10,000 for the performance, he gave up other performances and the marketing that comes along with those performances to play Carla's event. In the event Carla cancels the event, she will have to pay Toby $25,000. This liquidated damages clause may be enforceable as it reflects the amount calculated to compensate Toby for the loss of revenue, marketing, and other opportunity costs associated with playing the event.

In sales contracts, liquidated damages must be reasonable in light of:

- the anticipated or actual harm caused by the breach,
- the difficulties of proof of loss, and
- the inconvenience or lack of feasibility of otherwise obtaining an adequate remedy.

- *Example*: Mitchell enters into a contract to sell goods to Cameron for $1,000. Cameron intends to resell the goods to individual customers at a substantial profit. Mitchell is the only provider of the goods in the area and Cameron is paying a premium. The contract provides for liquidated damages in the amount of $2,000 if Mitchell does not perform. This amount is an estimate of the damages that Cameron will suffer from not having the goods to resell.

What are nominal damages?

Nominal damages are represented by a small amount awarded by the court to the plaintiff for a breach of contract that causes no financial injury to the plaintiff. Generally, nominal damages evidence the wrongful conduct of a party. Nominal damages, as the name indicates, are nominal in amount. A typical nominal damages award may be $1 or $10. Nominal damages can be important as they can be used to support an award of punitive damages in tort.

- *Example*: Billy enters into a contract with Karen to cut her grass. Billy fails to cut the grass and Karen is forced to hire someone else for the same price. While Karen did not suffer any expectation or consequential damages from Karen's breach, he is upset and sues Karen. The court may award nominal damages to demonstrate that Karen did wrong.

What are punitive damages?

Punitive damages, as the name implies, are used to punish a party. Punitive damages are rarely awarded in contract disputes. If, however, the conduct by a party is intentional and egregious, the court may award punitive damages in a tort action collateral to the contract claim. Punitive damages are particularly appropriate when there is evidence of fraud.

- *Example*: ABC, Inc., produces a part that is used in the driving mechanism of automobiles. In the production of the part, ABC realizes that the part may cause a defect in the steering column. ABC proceeds to market and sells the part to auto manufacturers. After a couple of years, individuals driving these cars have accidents and are injured as a result of the faulty part installed in the vehicle. These individuals initiate a class action against ABC. The jury finds ABC liable and awards $10 million dollars in compensatory damages to those injured. The jury also recommends punitive damages in the amount of $150 million dollars.

What is restitution?

Restitution is an equitable remedy whereby a court awards funds to a party to prevent the unfair gain or unjust enrichment of the other party. Use of this doctrine is common in situations where the breaching party receives a benefit by breaching the contract at the expense of the other party. An award of restitution may be appropriate even if the non-breaching party did not suffer losses as a result of the breach. The damages are generally calculated as the value of the benefit received by a party.

- *Example*: Arnold is a subcontractor who provides electrical services. Garth is a general contractor who regularly employs Arnold. Garth enters into a contract to construct a building for Ethan's business. Midway through the project, Garth gets into a conflict with Ethan and abandons the project. At this point Arnold has completed most of the electrical work. Garth refuses to pay Arnold because Ethan refuses to pay Garth for the work. While there is no contract between Ethan and Arnold, Ethan has received a benefit at Arnold's expense. Arnold may be able to bring an action against Ethan for restitution.

- *Note*: Restitution may be available in cases where there is no breach of contract. Examples of situations where restitution may be available in the absence of a breach of contract include: when value has been transferred but the contract is unenforceable, void, voidable; or when duties under the contract are discharged through some contractual excuse. The purpose of restitution is to prevent unjust enrichment by one party.

What is specific performance?

Specific performance is where a court orders the parties to consummate the transaction or complete the performance that is the subject of the contract. Specific performance may be appropriate where other forms of remedies cannot adequately compensate the party's loss. Specific performance is a common remedy when the contract involves the sale of unique goods (such as works of art) or real estate.

- *Example*: Marco enters into a contract to sell Pillar an original painting by Pablo Picasso. Before consummating the sale, Marco decides that he does not want to part with the work of art and backs out of the sale. Pillar sues Marco. There is a limited market for old masterpieces and the court is unable to ascertain damages based on the value of the painting. Because monetary damages will not remedy Pillar's loss, the court order's Marco to sell the painting to Pillar pursuant to the terms of the contract.

- *Note*: Specific performance is generally not available in personal service contracts. If Pillar contracted with Marco to paint a portrait, then the court would generally not order Marco to perform the obligations under the contract.

What is rescission?

Rescission is an equitable remedy where a court unwinds a contract. Basically, the contract is cancelled as if it never existed. If a new contract is not imputed, rescission requires each party to return the consideration given the other. Rescission is commonly ordered in fraud or misrepresentation cases.

- *Example:* Cliff defrauds Olivia into entering a contract to lease a timeshare in the Bahamas. Olivia sues Cliff to recover the money she paid him under the contract. If the court determines that fraud exists, the court may rescind the contract. The court will likely also order Cliff to pay restitution to Olivia to put her in the same position she was in before entering into the contract.

What is reformation?

Reformation is the rewriting of the contract to reflect the actual (or original) intent of the parties. This is common when the parties have an honest misunderstanding that detriments both parties to the contract.

- *Example*: Darla enters into a contract to supply cement to Michelle's construction company. Both parties are unaware that the contract calls for the wrong type of cement. The price for the incorrect cement is higher than that of the desired cement. When Darla realizes the error, she attempts to force Michelle to purchase the higher-priced, incorrect cement. In this case, the court will likely reform the contract to reflect the original intentions of the parties. Of course, Michelle will have to prove that there was a mutual mistake in the formation of the contract. This may be done with the introduction of parole (outside) evidence.

Does the non-breaching party have a duty to mitigate the amount of damages?

Yes. The non-breaching party has a duty to mitigate damages to the extent reasonable. This will depend upon the nature and context of the contract.

- *Example*: Tom leases a building from Dave. Tom is unable to make the payments and defaults on the lease. Tom moves out and the building is vacant. Dave has a duty to attempt to mitigate the damages suffered under the contract.

Conclusion

You have reached the end and now have a thorough understanding of the major legal issues affecting contracts. Hopefully, this text will prove useful to you as a manager or entrepreneur building your business. If you have any comments or feedback, please contact me at www.TheBusinessProfessor.com.

Thank you.

Jason M. Gordon, JD, MBA, LLM

Made in the USA
Charleston, SC
15 February 2015